Hidden Profits in YOUR MORTGAGE

Hidden Profits in YOUR MORTGAGE

The Smart-Money Guide to Canadian Home Ownership

Alan Silverstein

Stoddart

First published in 1985 by Stoddart Publishing
34 Lesmill Road
Toronto, Canada
M3B 2T6

Second Printing - December 1985
Third Printing - August 1986

CANADIAN CATALOGUING IN PUBLICATION DATA

Silverstein, Alan Gary, 1951
    Hidden profits in your mortgage
ISBN 0-7737-2045-6
1. Mortgages - Canada. 2. Housing - Canada - Finance. I. Title.
HD1379.S55 1985   332.7 '2   C85-098150-6

The Mortgage Value Tables appearing on pages 186 and 187 are reprinted with the permission of Computo Facts, Willowdale, Ont., from their book Monthly Mortgage Tables .

Printed in Canada

Contents

Preface

The 1980s have been called the "decade of consumer awareness." The public is pushing for more and more answers about forces affecting their daily lives.

Nowhere is this more evident than in the area of mortgage financing. For years, Canadian borrowers quietly and virtually automatically accepted the terms of mortgages presented to them by financial institutions. Rarely were any questions raised as to how appropriate those terms were to a borrower's personal circumstances. When interest rates began to rise, borrowers' eyes began to open to the enormous sums of money — after-tax funds, no less — that had to be earned to finance a mortgage. The demand for advice as to how to pare down enormous interest costs was on!

This book has been written with these thoughts in mind. Its goal is twofold. The first is to make borrowers more comfortable and at ease when negotiating a mortgage loan. This is essential if the most advantageous overall mortgage package, personalized to a borrower's needs and financial situation, is to be obtained. Whether the loan is arranged to purchase a home or to refinance an existing loan, borrowers must embark on a fact-finding expedition by asking pertinent questions and demanding thorough answers. Only in this way can sound, thoughtful decisions be made which deal with tens of thousands of the borrower's hard-earned dollars. The best negotiations are conducted from a position of strength. Borrowers can approach a lender head-high knowing that they qualify for a mortgage, and that the property to be mortgaged qualifies as well. The days of going cap-in-hand to a lender, grovelling for a mortgage, are over!

Second, borrowers will be introduced to a number of different methods that exist to reduce the high interest costs involved in carrying a mortgage. As "The Mortgage Magician," I will show you a number of "tricks" to make some of those interest costs disappear. These tricks are different examples of what I call the POPS principle — Paying Off the Principal Sooner. Look for the mortgage that is tops in POPS — it can be the most profitable game in town. POPS is an inexpensive way, as well, to take advantage of those hidden profits in a home mortgage. Those who gain most from this book will convert their anxiety over their mortgages into positive action, to hack away at the high interest costs.

Unless otherwise noted, examples provided are for blended payment mortgages, with fixed interest rates. The mortgage is calculated semi-annually, not in advance, the standard method by which Canadian mortgages are calculated. While interest rates may vary over the amortized life of the loan, a constant interest rate is assumed for comparative purposes, unless otherwise noted.

By design, no financial institutions have been specifically named in the book. Change happens so quickly in the area of mortgage financing that keeping pace with the latest developments is a difficult task. Instead of comparing one lender's product against another's by name, the features of mortgages currently available in the marketplace will be clearly explained. In this fashion, the overall package offered by one lender can be compared with that offered by another. Changes made by lenders to their products over time will not automatically make the book out of date.

I am a lawyer, not a banker, not an economist. I have no control over interest *rates* — I too am subject to their fluctuations as a home owner. But I advocate strongly the POPS principle, to substantially reduce the interest *costs* paid by borrowers, without in any way changing or affecting the interest rate charged by lenders.

My experiences as a real estate lawyer as well as personal experience have been drawn upon. The more important experiences, however, are those encountered by Canadians every day when arranging, prepaying or refinancing their mortgages. I would be very interested to learn more about concerns and problems that the Canadian public has faced in these areas. My publisher has graciously indicated that mail addressed to me c/o Stoddart Publishing, 30 Lesmill Road, Toronto, Ontario, M3B 2T6, will be forwarded to me. Please include a copy of any relevant documents that might help in my understanding of the situation you have encountered.

Acknowledgements

This book is like a dream — an opportunity to put on paper and express to the Canadian public the ideas milling about in my head for the past 10 years on mortgage financing. I am indebted to those people who have helped make this book. My appreciation goes out to the four fine people who helped type the manuscript — my secretaries, Joan de Swart and Donna Boisselle, my friend, Elaine Haft, and especially to my brother-in-law, Danny J. Rosenzweig. At Stoddart Publishing, I would like to thank my editor, Don Loney; my publisher, Ed Carson; and senior vice-president, Nelson Doucet. Special thanks, as well, to a good friend, Ellen Roseman, who helped open a number of doors. My last thank you is reserved for those people to whom this book is dedicated: my dear wife Hannah, and my wonderful sons, Elliott and Darryl. Without their unfailing support and understanding, the realization of my dream would not have come true.

1

An Introduction To Mortgage Financing

Probably no word in the English language strikes more fear into the hearts of mortal men and women than the term "mortgage" (or, as it is known in some land registration systems, "charge"). For generations, people have approached borrowing money on a mortgage as gleefully as they would taking castor oil. For most people who own or are about to buy a home, mortgages are a necessary evil. Lenders know the rules of the game called mortgage financing. It's high time that borrowers learned both the rules as well as the strategies of the game in order to play it competitively. While lenders have an advantage, since they can change the rules of the game, this should not deter borrowers. After all, the money they save will be their own!

Not all mortgages are created equal. With the vast number of variations in mortgage products available from different lenders today, it's amazing any similarities exist at all. Like hair shampoo, the different products all claim to be the "best" for the consumer. While it is easy to switch from a brand of shampoo if dissatisfied with its performance, that is not the case with a mortgage. The cost of acquiring a lender's product is usually exceeded by the cost of discarding it.

"Shop around" — a catchy expression that applies to almost all consumer activities today. Negotiating a mortgage is no different. There is so much more to a mortgage than its interest rate, that the interest rate should not be the only factor considered when shopping for a mortgage. A prepayment penalty incurred to pay off a closed mortgage in midterm, for example, could mean that a closed low interest rate mortgage could cost more overall than one with a higher interest rate that is open.

With the vast variation in mortgage terms among mortgage lenders, buyers and home owners (when refinancing) *must* enquire about these factors as diligently as they would investigate the options on a car. The nature of the mortgage market is changing. No longer can it be assumed that buyers will automatically want to assume a seller's mortgage on closing. An ill-prepared vendor in this situation may have to pay thousands of dollars as a penalty. With interest rates remaining higher than the historical average, short-term mortgages becoming a trend and different variations on the mortgage theme hitting the market on a regular basis, borrowers must become "educated consumers." Once the principles are understood, the potential benefits are enormous.

A recent trend in mortgage financing has been to view mortgages more and more as personal loans, although they are secured by land. "Due on sale" clauses, more liberalized prepayment terms and new payment schemes, such as weekly mortgages, are all signs that lenders are increasingly refining their mortgage products with the borrower and his ability to pay the loan in mind. Knowing this, borrowers should ensure that the overall mortgage package fits their financial position. Just as a tailor-made suit should fit better than one off the rack, so too with today's mortgages. A tailor-made mortgage will save the borrower substantial sums of money — after-tax dollars — and will remove the albatross of mortgage payments sooner.

It's time to put fear and worry aside, and to start feeling comfortable about mortgages.

2

Mortgage Jargon

Tourists, when strangers in a strange land, always feel more comfortable when they can speak the language of the locals. Here is a short lesson in the language of the mortgage world.

Mortgage

A legal contract, registered against the title to property, providing security to the lender for the repayment of a loan, is called a mortgage. It is derived from two French words, "mort" (dead) and "gage" (pledge). Once the loan is paid off, the need for this security terminates. "You paid me back, I've got my bread, the pledge is dead," the lender said.

If I borrow $10 from a friend, he would want written proof that I owe him the money — an IOU in other words. If home owners look at mortgages as a "fancy form of an IOU," borrowing on a mortgage is a lot easier to swallow. Of course, a mortgage is a more elaborate form of an IOU than a mere scrap of paper. It is registered against the title to the borrower's property, and it provides stated rights and remedies to the lender if there is default. Still, it basically provides proof of a debt and security for the lender that the debt will be repaid on time.

When a loan is arranged, the borrower gives a mortgage, or mortgages his property, in return for the money received. When the borrower returns the money to the lender, the lender returns the mortgage document to the borrower together with a receipt, usually called a discharge. This is registered against the title to the property, in order for the existence of the mortgage to be deleted from title.

A mortgage loan looks like this:

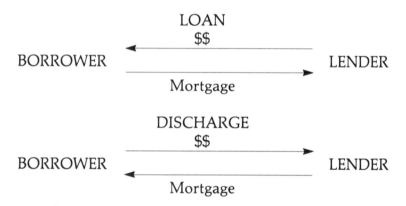

Mortgagor — The borrower. Remember — "or" owes — the mortga*gor* owes the money.
Mortgagee — The lender.
Principal — The amount initially borrowed from the lender.
Interest — The lender's charge for the use of the money supplied to the borrower.

Equity
The amount of the home owner's interest in the property is called equity. It is the difference between the fair market value of the property and the outstanding mortgages. A home owner's equity increases with each pay-

ment of principal in a blended mortgage, even if ever so slightly. A home owner's equity will also increase or decrease based on any change in the fair market value of the property.

The best way to look at equity is to view a house as an elastic pie — one that can either shrink or grow. Assume Ron and Cheryl's house (and therefore the pie) is worth $100,000. If they have financed their house with a $70,000 mortgage, the lender owns the $70,000 piece of the pie, while Ron and Cheryl's share (their equity) is $30,000. If the house does not change in value, every dollar of principal paid by Ron and Cheryl would increase their share of the pie while similarly reducing the lender's interest in the property. Principal payments adding up to $250 over a year mean Ron and Cheryl's share of the pie (or their equity in the property) is now $30,250, the lender's share being reduced to $69,750.

Whatever happens to the value of the property affects only Ron and Cheryl's share of the pie. A drop in property value to $97,500 means their share of the pie or their equity is now $27,750 ($97,500 less the $69,750 owing to the lender). If the property rises in value to $102,000, they get the benefit of the $2,000 increase, meaning their equity is now $32,250 ($102,000 less the outstanding mortgage of $69,750).

Taking the elastic pie example a little further, if Ron and Cheryl need a $5,000 loan, and have equity of $32,250, they could arrange an "equity loan" for the $5,000. Equity loans are very common for home renovations and improvements, and are really nothing more than second mortgages. What they are doing is giving another lender (a second mortgagee) a $5,000 piece of the pie.

If the property is worth $102,000, and the amount of the two mortgages totals $74,750, the equity is reduced to $27,250. Once the $5,000 is repaid, Ron and Cheryl get that piece of the pie back, and their equity returns to $32,250, assuming nothing else has changed.

The priority of claims can be illustrated by picturing a totem pole worth $102,000. The first mortgagee is at the top, with a share of $69,750. Next comes the lender with the $5,000 second mortgage. At the bottom of the totem pole are Ron and Cheryl, with the remaining share.

Remember: (1) only the home owner's equity is affected by changes in the value of the house, and (2) the faster the principal is paid to the lender, the faster the purchaser's equity increases. Since most people aim for 100% equity, to own their homes "free and clear," playing POPS will accelerate this growth of equity.

Term

Do not confuse term with amortization: they are two totally unrelated concepts. The term for a mortgage is its life, plain and simple. Be it six months or five years, at the end of the mortgage term (its maturity), the entire amount outstanding on the mortgage is due and payable. After all, the contract is over. Canadian mortgages are called balloon mortgages for this reason. After making the fixed number of mortgage payments over the term of a mortgage, a "balloon" amount is due and owing to the lender at the end of the mortgage term. Three options are open to a borrower on the maturity of a loan — the 3 R's — (a) renew the loan with the existing lender; (b) refinance the loan by replacing it with a loan from a different lender; or (c) retire the loan by paying it off completely.

Amortization (sometimes just called the "am")

Latin in origin, it is derived from the expression "ad mortem," to the death. It represents the period of time that it would take if all blended mortgage payments were made punctually, with no prepayments and no late payments, for the loan to be fully retired. Looked at another way, a mortgage "self-destructs" at the end of the amortization period.

Once the principal and interest have been determined, the selection of an amortization is the last factor in calculating the amount of the monthly payment. Shorter amortization periods mean less interest is paid overall, although it also means a higher monthly payment. On a $50,000 loan at 13%, a 25-year amortization means monthly payments of $551.20. If the amortization is reduced to 20 years, the monthly payments would be $573.77, an increase of $22.56. A 15-year amortization would cost $621.52 monthly.

The standard amortization period for a mortgage is 25 years. In the United States, it is 30 years. Therefore, a three-year term/25-year amortization mortgage means that the life of the mortgage is three years, with the payments being calculated as if they would be made over a continuous 25-year period.

Older mortgage terms and amortization periods coincided. The good old NHA (National Housing Act) mortgage that covered so many of our parents' homes, had terms *and* amortizations of 25 years. Unfortunately, they died with the Edsel.

Lenders have what are called "amortization books" to tell them what the blended monthly payment will be for a certain principal amount, at a certain interest rate, at various amortizations. As helpful as these books are, they sometimes are relied upon too heavily, to the borrower's detriment.

Blended Payments

If principal is to be repaid each month, this can be achieved in two ways. Where a loan is "principal plus interest," a fixed amount of principal is repaid each month, together with interest on the outstanding balance. According to this "unblended" method, the largest and hardest payment to make comes the very first month. The interest component will be reduced in the future, reflecting the reduced outstanding principal. For example, a loan repayable $100 monthly principal plus interest at 13% calculated monthly will have a mortgage payment the first month of $641.67, made up of the $100 principal and $541.67 interest. In the second month the payment is reduced to $640.58 because the previous month's principal was reduced by $100.

Far more common, however, is the "blended" payment method. Here, the same amount of money, consisting of both a principal and an interest component, is paid to the lender each month during the term of the loan. The composition of the payment changes each month. More money is allocated to principal over time, while the amount of the payment allocated to interest falls accordingly, yet the monthly payment of principal and interest combined remains the same. Here too, though, the highest interest component is in the earliest years of the mortgage, although the payment is constant for the mortgage term.

Amortization Schedule (See Appendix B)

Figuring out exactly how much of a blended monthly payment is principal and how much of it is interest is extremely difficult. The same holds true for determining the exact amount outstanding on a mortgage at any given point in time. A computer printout, called an amortization schedule (or an "am" schedule), which is tailored to the mortgage, provides this information. At a nominal cost, one may be purchased from a number of computer services companies.

3

The Financial Side To Mortgages

Mortgages consist of four basic financial components: the principal, the interest rate, the amortization period and the payment. Select any three factors and the fourth is automatically determined. For a $50,000 mortgage at 13% per annum, amortized over 25 years, the payment is $551.20. If the amortization period were to be reduced to 20 years from 25, the corresponding change in the payment component would be an increase to $573.77 per month; the other two factors remain constant. Increase the principal to $60,000, and the payment will be $661.44 amortized over 25 years and $688.52 amortized over 20 years. The interplay of these four components is extremely important, especially when considering some of the POPS techniques.

When an apartment is leased, the tenant pays rent for the use of the suite for the month. Mortgage financing is no different. Interest is no more than rent paid by a borrower for the use of the lender's money for the month. Interest can only be charged on the amount of the principal outstanding at any point in time. The smaller the outstanding principal, the less interest that is payable. The faster the principal is repaid, the sooner that interest will no longer be chargeable.

As can be seen from the am schedule in Appendix B, mortgages are heavily front-end loaded. By far the largest component of the blended payment in the early stages of a mortgage term is interest. Imagine paying $551.20 to a lender for the first month's mortgage payment, and only increasing in the equity in the property by $23.65. The second month's principal portion increases — but ever so slightly — by only 25 cents. In fact, after making mortgage payments for one full year, totalling $6,614.40, only $300.82 has gone toward the principal. In other words, over 95% of the payments on this loan in its first year went to interest!

The overall cost of the interest on this mortgage, otherwise known as the cost of borrowing, is not overly appealing either. Assuming the interest rate did not change over 25 years, the interest costs on a $50,000 loan would be $115,367.71. The $50,000 principal also needs to be repaid as well! Financing a loan costs over twice as much as the amount of the loan itself. No wonder Canadians are up in arms about mortgage costs!

Anything that can help reduce these incredible interest costs is a cause for rejoicing. I call it the POPS principle. Borrowers who pay off their principal sooner will save enormous sums of money, making the benefits of playing the POPS game virtually unbelievable. Remember as well that POPS saves after-tax dollars for Canadians — money on which income taxes have already been paid. In gross income terms, the savings could be a further one-third or more! Stupendous!

4

Canadian vs.
American Mortgages

Although sometimes it is difficult to do, we Canadians like to emphasize how different we are from our American friends. In the area of mortgage financing, the basic concepts and legalities of a mortgage are the same in both countries. This reflects the British tradition that forms the backbone of both societies. Substantial distinctions do exist between Canadian and American mortgages, though, dealing mainly with the charging and collecting of interest. The differences are so important that American publications and advertising seen in Canada can mislead and confuse Canadian readers. In some respects Canadian mortgages are better than American mortgages, and vice versa: "You win some, you lose some." Here are the key areas where Canadian and American mortgages diverge:

1. Canadian mortgages generally are calculated semi-annually (or half-yearly) because of stipulations in the *Interest Act of Canada.* American mortgages are calculated monthly. Borrowers benefit from the Canadian position, because the annual effective interest rate is lower for a loan calculated semi-annually.

2. Canadian mortgages are payable at the end of the payment period. American mortgages are payable at the start of that period. Again, Canadian borrowers benefit, because they, rather than the lender, have the money in their possession to earn additional money during that time. Score another one for the Maple Leaf.

3. Amortizations in Canada traditionally have been 25-year periods. American amortizations normally run to 30 years. Longer amortizations mean lower monthly payments, *but* higher overall interest costs. The name of the game is to reduce the outstanding amortization, not to increase it. A benefit to Canadians.

4. The maximum mortgage term available to Canadian borrowers is five years. Canadian financial institutions hold the mortgages as part of their portfolio of assets. American mortgages are funded differently. Two federal government agencies known as "Fannie Mae" and "Freddy Mac" act as a secondary market for many American mortgages, permitting longer mortgage terms for borrowers, often as long as the amortization itself. These long-term, self-amortizing mortgages are a distinct benefit to American borrowers.

5. Interest deductability. Mortgage interest costs are fully deductable from other income in the United States. No deduction for mortgage interest costs exists in Canada, except in limited circumstances. The 1979 Budget presented by former Prime Minister Joe Clark would have permitted mortgage interest deductability. Since then, little has been heard on the topic. How to make mortgage interest deductable under the appropriate circumstances is discussed in chapter 38.

The current state of Canadian income tax law means that mortgage payments are made from after-tax dollars (money on which income tax has already been paid). This means the amount of income that must be earned to finance the mortgage is considerably higher. Understanding and applying the POPS principle in order for Canadians to save money is a must.

When the benefits and drawbacks between Canadian and American mortgages are compared, it's a draw.

5

Does The Property Qualify?

When lenders are deciding whether to loan money secured by a mortgage, two different requirements must be satisfied: the property and its ability to protect the loan (the security, or the property requirement), and the borrower's dependability and his financial ability to repay the loan (the covenant, or income requirement). The key element here is determining whether the borrower's income will qualify for a mortgage loan. Conversely, how large a mortgage can be arranged, based on the borrower's income? This is discussed in the next chapter.

The factors discussed in both this and the following chapter apply equally whether a loan is being arranged to finance the purchase of a home, or whether a home owner is refinancing an existing loan.

Generally speaking, home buyers should pay as much money on closing as they can afford. This will mean a smaller mortgage will have to be carried. In addition, the largest monthly payment possible should be made. The overall effect of doing this will be to substantially reduce the overall interest cost for the house. It also makes the transaction a more desirable investment opportunity for the lender.

The maximum amount that lenders will loan depends upon the value of the property. To establish this, lenders will order an appraisal of the property. A qualified professional land appraiser will go to the property, investigate it, research the market for the value of similar properties in the same general area that have been recently sold, and then advise the lender of its appraised value. This is *not*, however, a home inspection.

Usually the appraisal will show the value of the land and the value of the house separately — important information to have when arranging insurance on the property. The appraiser will consider a property's location, zoning by-laws, the condition of the building, how well the area is serviced by the municipality, lot size, and the upkeep of homes in the same neighborhood.

The appraisal should show that the price paid for a property at the time it is being acquired is "in the ball park." After all, no one wants to learn that he has overpaid for a property. A purchase at slightly under the appraised value will be welcome news to a buyer. Try to get a copy of the appraisal, for it contains a world of information about the property and similar properties in the area. Not all lenders will release the appraisal to borrowers. Yet when borrowers (whether on a purchase or on a refinancing) learn they are paying as much as $200 for the appraisal, payable "up front" on submitting the mortgage application, they rightly feel entitled to a copy of the report at the very least.

Check the lender's charges for the appraisal *before* making a mortgage application. Some lenders' "appraisal" fees cover the cost of the application as well; others will charge a separate application fee.

Once the appraisal is back, the lender can decide whether the property qualifies for the loan. Lenders generally, and institutional lenders by law, will not grant a "conventional" mortgage for more than 75% of the appraised value of the property. This is the "75%

Rule" or "loan to value ratio" referred to by most lenders. A conventional mortgage, then, requires that the borrower's equity in the property be at least 25% of its appraised value. This is important to keep in mind, especially when purchasing a home. The purchase price and the amount paid by the purchaser from his own resources on closing will largely determine whether the property will provide adequate security for the lender. For a property appraised at $80,000, the maximum amount that can be secured by a conventional mortgage is $60,000. If a mortgage for more than 75% of the appraised value is required, meaning the home owner's equity is less than 25%, the loan is considered to be "high ratio." For the loan to be granted, "mortgage payment insurance" must be arranged on the *entire* mortgage amount (and not just the portion exceeding 75% of the appraised value), guaranteeing the monthly payments to the lender. This type of insurance is available through a private insurer, the Mortgage Insurance Company of Canada, or CMHC, Central Mortgage and Housing Corporation. CMHC also provides NHA loans. The insurance fee, which is paid in addition to the application/appraisal fee, could be quite substantial — up to 2½% of the amount of the principal. This fee is usually added to the amount of the mortgage. More information on this type of mortgage insurance appears in chapter 33.

When buying a house, if your down payment is less than 25% of the purchase price, you should get the most up-to-date information on NHA and high-ratio loans. Depending on the circumstances, up to 95% of the appraised value of a property, up to specified limits, can be lent by a financial institution if the appropriate insurance coverage is arranged.

In some cases, MICC/CMHC fees can be avoided by

splitting the high-ratio loan into a conventional first mortgage and a second mortgage. See chapter 29 for a discussion of second mortgages.

Knowing that the property test has been satisfied, how do the borrowers stand up? Is there sufficient income to assure the lender that the loan will be repaid without difficulty? If so, then the borrower should have no problem in obtaining the mortgage.

6

Do The Borrowers Qualify?

In the last chapter, the property and its ability to properly secure a loan was considered. In this chapter, the lender's concerns about the borrower and his ability to finance the loan are examined.

Uncertainty as to whether a mortgage will be granted accounts for much of the anxiety associated with mortgage financing. Home buyers with an offer conditional on financing are on pins and needles until learning whether the mortgage applied for will be granted. Home owners wishing to refinance an existing loan face the same problem when awaiting mortgage approval. If borrowers knew in advance that they would qualify for a mortgage, much of the anguish they face while waiting for mortgage approval could be reduced or even eliminated. Borrowers could also confidently shop for the mortgage terms that are best for them.

Help is on the way! Read on.

Mortgage lenders want extensive information about a borrower and his financial background. A typical mortgage application form, like any type of a loan application form, requires a personal net worth statement consisting of a detailed list of assets and liabilities; sources of income; employment particulars; income information, often to be confirmed by a letter from the employer or by providing an income tax return; and credit references. An authorization for a credit check may have to be signed. Especially on home purchases, a letter may have to be produced (an "equity" letter), from the home buyer's bank, showing that sufficient funds are available to satisfy the balance due on closing. Buyers should also take a copy of the offer to the lender. Where a purchase and sale is involved, copies of both offers should be taken to the lender to establish the equity from the sale of the existing house. After all, lenders want to ensure that the proposed mortgage coupled with the buyer's own resources will be sufficient to enable the transaction to close. Note that although a request for a Social Insurance Number may be made, borrowers are under no legal obligation to provide it.

The amounts sought in most mortgage applications usually exceed the loan limits of the local branch of a financial institution, so the application must be processed by and approval come from a regional or head office. This takes time. Be prepared for delays of a week or more — be patient. Although the decision-making power is outside the hands of the local branch's loans officer, borrowers should stay in regular contact with that official, especially if a condition on financing must be waived on a home purchase. During this period, a thorough credit check of the borrower is conducted to verify the accuracy of the credit information provided.

The lender's greatest concern about the borrower is that his gross income be large enough and sufficiently stable to handle the costs associated with owning a house and carrying a mortgage. In deciding whether to grant a mortgage loan, institutional lenders consider what percentage principal, interest and taxes (and maintenance for condominium mortgages) represents of a potential borrower's gross income. Usually, but not always, the combined gross incomes of both a husband and wife as borrowers are considered. The conventional rule is that these items should not exceed 30% of the borrowers' gross incomes. This is the Gross Debt Service, or GDS ratio, that lenders speak of. Another calculation, called the TDS, or Total Debt Service ratio, looks at the percentage of gross annual income needed to service *all* debt payments — house, personal loan, car loan and so on. The total debt payments should not exceed 37% to 40% of the borrowers' gross incomes, depending on the lender. These percentages are not etched in stone, and are subject to change and to non-observance, in appropriate circumstances.

Most borrowers would like to know as early as possible if their incomes qualify for a mortgage loan. This is especially important for home buyers with offers conditional on arranging financing who are awaiting "word," as if it came from on high! An easy way to calculate the amount of gross income needed to qualify for a mortgage is to combine the monthly mortgage payments, amortized over 25 years, with one-twelfth of the realty taxes and the monthly condominium maintenance payment, if applicable. Multiply the total by 40. If the gross income exceeds this amount, the GDS ratio has been satisfied. Simple! Easy piece of mind! Income qualifications can be determined in seconds!

For example, if the mortgage payments will run $600 a month, the estimated annual taxes are $1,200 or $100 a month, and the property is not a condominium, then the gross income needed to service the loan is $600 + $100 x 40, or $28,000. Borrowers with gross incomes exceeding this amount satisfy the GDS ratio. This is the "30%" or "times 40" rule lenders refer to.

Following is a chart showing the monthly payment

that will be required per thousand dollars of a mortgage loan at various interest rates and at various amortizations. Use this chart to calculate the approximate cost of financing a loan. To determine the monthly payment for a loan, look at the 25-year amortization column, as well as the quoted interest rate. Multiply the figure by the amount of the mortgage (in thousands of dollars) being considered to determine the approximate monthly payment. For example, if the quoted interest rate is 13% and a $50,000 mortgage is needed, amortized over 25 years, multiply 11.02 by 50 to get a figure of $551 (the actual payment, when properly calculated, is $551.20).

Add to this figure one-twelfth of the annual realty taxes and multiply the total by 40 to see what income level is needed to finance the loan. In other words, if taxes were $110.00 monthly, the income threshold is $661 times 40 or $26,440.

Calculate the gross incomes needed to service a mortgage, based on different amounts at different interest rates, in the space below. The formula is:

Monthly mortgage payment for a mortgage of $_____ at _____%	+	Estimated monthly taxes	+	Monthly condominium maintenance payment	x 40 =	Gross Income Needed

From this, it is easy to see how higher interest rates eliminate potential buyers from the market. For a property with annual taxes of $120 a month, a buyer with a

Calculating the Monthly Payment for a $1,000 Loan at Various Interest Rates at Various Amortizations

Calculated semi-annually not in advance

AMORTIZATION	15	20	25	30
INTEREST RATE		$		
10%	10.62	9.52	8.95	8.63
10.5%	10.92	9.83	9.28	8.98
11%	11.21	10.16	9.63	9.40
11.5%	11.51	10.48	9.97	9.70
12%	11.82	10.81	10.32	10.06
12.5%	12.12	11.14	10.67	10.43
13%	12.43	11.48	11.02	10.80
13.5%	12.74	11.81	11.38	11.17
14%	13.06	12.15	11.74	11.54
14.5%	13.37	12.49	12.10	11.92
15%	13.69	12.84	12.46	12.29
15.5%	14.01	13.18	12.83	12.66
16%	14.33	13.53	13.19	13.04
16.5%	14.66	13.88	13.56	13.42
17%	14.99	14.23	13.93	13.79
17.5%	15.32	14.59	14.29	14.17
18%	15.65	14.94	14.66	14.55
18.5%	15.98	15.30	15.03	14.93
19%	16.31	15.66	15.41	15.31
19.5%	16.65	16.01	15.78	15.69
20%	16.99	16.38	16.15	16.06

$50,000 mortgage at 13% would need $26,848 in income to qualify for the mortgage. At 14%, the income would have to be $28,277. The income needed to maintain a 15% mortgage would be $29,723.

Now look at matters from a different perspective. How large a mortgage can a borrower arrange? The gross incomes of the borrowers and the applicable interest rates would determine this question. Frank and Carol have a $20,000 down payment to buy a house, and gross incomes of $35,000. Although their income base is good, their down payment would only permit a conventional mortgage of $60,000, allowing them to purchase an $80,000 home. If they wanted to go "high-ratio," a house could be bought in the range between $82,000 and $95,000, depending on the interest rates. This range is based on their $20,000 down payment and the size of the mortgage permitted by the income qualification rules, as described below.

Using the "times 40" rule, Frank and Carol's incomes would allow a monthly mortgage payment for principal, interest and taxes of $875. (Instead of multiplying the total mortgage payment by 40, divide their gross incomes by 40.) Assuming a $100 monthly tax component, $775 still is available for the principal and interest portion of a mortgage payment. Looking at the 25-year amortization column from the chart on page 37, dividing $755 by the payment for 12% ($10.32) would show that Frank and Carol could carry a mortgage of approximately $75,000 at 12%. Dividing the $775 monthly payment by the figure at 13% would show that a $70,000 mortgage could be carried at that interest rate. Repeating this for 14% and 15% would indicate that mortgages of $66,000 and $62,000 could be carried at those rates respectively.

Financing a conventional mortgage for $60,000 on an $80,000 purchase, then, should be no problem for Frank and Carol. A slightly more expensive house could be bought as well, financed by a high-ratio mortgage, provided interest rates remained reasonable.

To calculate the maximum mortgage that can be carried in a given situation, complete the following calculations:

Divide: Gross Income by 40 = Gross Monthly Payment
Deduct: 1/12th of the annual taxes
Difference = Maximum amount available for principal and interest payments

Use this figure to calculate the largest mortgage available at various interest rates. (See the chart on page 37.)

Frank and Carol's chart would look like this:

$35,000 ÷ 40 =	$875
Deduct:	100
Difference:	$775

Interest Rate	Maximum Mortgage Permitted Based on Income	
10%	$ 86,600	Note: Divide the "difference" by the factor in the 25-year amortization column for the desired interest rate to determine the maximum mortgage permitted (i.e., $775 ÷ $10.32 is $75,000 for a 12% mortgage).
11%	$ 80,500	
12%	$ 75,000	
13%	$ 70,000	
14%	$ 66,000	
15%	$ 62,000	

Make the appropriate calculations below:

$ _____   ÷ 40   = $ _____
Deduct: 1/12th annual taxes _____
Difference: $_____

At 10% a mortgage of $ can be arranged.
At 11% a mortgage of $ can be arranged.
At 12% a mortgage of $ can be arranged.
At 13% a mortgage of $ can be arranged.
At 14% a mortgage of $ can be arranged.
At 15% a mortgage of $ can be arranged.

Borrowers who discover at this stage, even before a formal mortgage application is submitted, that they and the property will qualify for the loan, they can begin their comparative shopping for the best overall package of mortgage terms.

7

Where Can Borrowers Go To Get A Mortgage?

Most people are familiar with the obvious sources for mortgage loans; these are the institutional lenders that most borrowers think of first, namely banks, trust companies, insurance companies and credit unions. A number of other sources do exist which are worth exploring under the appropriate circumstances. Buyers of resale properties should note that the number of options open to them greatly exceeds those for borrowers refinancing their mortgage.

I. General

Mortgage Brokers

Mortgage brokers are like real estate agents — matchmakers — in that they bring together lenders and borrowers. They serve the residential real estate market in a number of ways, and charge a fee for their service. On home purchases, where time is a major factor, they are able to arrange a mortgage to satisfy a condition on financing. If the situation is sound both from a security and covenant point of view, some brokers will commit on the loan virtually immediately, and place the loan with a specific lender afterwards. By dealing constantly with a number of lenders, both private and institutional, brokers can help get the best possible rate and terms.

Some home owners also like to use brokers when refinancing existing property. Much of the paperwork and shopping for terms is left to the broker.

Mortgage brokers are helpful to borrowers, whether purchasing or refinancing, who would not qualify for a loan with a conventional financial institution. The Gross Debt Ratio could be slightly too high, the borrower's equity in the property could be too small, or the borrower's credit rating may not be AAA.

While the fee charged by brokers depends on a number of factors, such as the nature of the transaction, whether a first or second mortgage is involved, and the terms of the mortgage obtained, brokers do charge anywhere from 1% to 2% of the principal amount of the mortgage for their services — sometimes more on smaller loans. Lesser fees are often charged when a mortgage is arranged with an institutional lender in a purchase situation. While brokers do provide a valuable service, most noticeably in purchase transactions, learn what their charges and fees will be at the outset. If you require a broker's services, it is wise to budget ahead of time.

Private Funds

Many lawyers have lender clients looking to invest funds in mortgages. To be competitive, private lenders may offer concessions to borrowers — slightly-below-market interest rates, more liberal prepayment privileges, and so on.

II. Buyers of Resale Properties

Buyers of resale properties have three different ways of financing their purchase. A combination of methods is possible if more than one mortgage is involved:

- the buyer arranges his own mortgage
- the buyer assumes the existing mortgage
- the seller "takes back" a mortgage for the unpaid balance of the purchase price.

A word to buyers — proceed with extreme caution. The wording of the "mortgage" clause in the offer will have a great bearing on the content of mortgages in the second and third categories. "If it is not in the offer, it won't be in the mortgage." Great care therefore is needed in drafting the mortgage financing clause in an offer.

The Buyer Arranges His Own Mortgage

Rarely does a buyer have a firm commitment for a mortgage when the offer is signed. Most offers will be made "conditional" upon the purchaser arranging satisfactory financing within a specified time. From the seller's point of view, he does not care where the money comes from — whether it is begged, borrowed or stolen — since the transaction between the buyer and the seller is all cash. The choice of a lender, however, is obviously all important to the purchaser/borrower.

Even before submitting an offer, the purchaser should hold preliminary discussions with a potential lender. Also, chapters 5 and 6 should be reviewed to ensure that property and income qualifications can be satisfied. Buyers should be able to learn informally if they will qualify for a mortgage if the offer were to be accepted. No one needs unpleasant surprises. No one wants to submit a conditional offer only to learn later that he cannot get a mortgage to complete the transaction.

Buyers should allow at least a week and preferably two to obtain mortgage approval. Paperwork does take time!

The Buyer Assumes the Existing Mortgage

Here the buyer assumes the rights and obligations of the seller under the mortgage already registered and outstanding. The amount of the mortgage assumed is deducted from the purchase price that has to be paid on closing.

By assuming the existing mortgage, buyers often are able to save money because the interest rate is below the current market rate. A mortgage like this, if assumable, is a selling feature of the house as much as the lot size and interior layout.

Before an offer is prepared, the agent should verify with the lender: the amount outstanding on the loan both today *and* at the anticipated closing date, the interest rate, the payments, the remaining term of the mortgage, whether taxes are paid through the lender, what the prepayment privileges are, and whether the mortgage is assumable, non-assumable, or assumable with the lender's approval. If prior approval from the lender is needed, the purchaser should make the offer conditional on obtaining the approval. Without this prior verification, a buyer could agree to assume an existing mortgage only to find out later that the terms are totally different than anticipated.

Assuming an existing mortgage, even if lender approval is required, is a fast, easy and cheap way to get a mortgage. No appraisal fee, application fee or legal fees have to be paid. The mortgage is already registered on title — all the buyer has to do is make the payments after closing.

On the other hand, the terms of the mortgage are nonnegotiable. What you see is what you get. If the remaining term is short, the loan may have to be renegotiated shortly. Do not assume the mortgage will automatically be renewed, especially in private lender situations. This could lead to additional expenses in the near future.

The Seller "Takes Back" a Mortgage for the Unpaid Balance of the Purchase Price

To sell a property, some sellers will help the purchaser buy the house by providing financing through a vendor-take-back (or VTB) mortgage — be it a first, second or third mortgage. Alan and Hannah are planning on buying a house worth $90,000, and have saved $20,000. If they can assume the outstanding first mortgage of $60,000, the $10,000 difference could be secured by a VTB second mortgage. An alternative is for the vendor to take back a $60,000 first mortgage, leaving Alan and Hannah to arrange their own $10,000 second mortgage.

VTB mortgages are another cheap source of money. Again they are easy, quick and cheap to arrange. No credit checks, no appraisal and application fees, no legal fees. Once the offer is signed, the buyer has been approved for the loan.

The terms of the VTB mortgage must be spelled out clearly in the offer. Crucial terms include the principal, the interest rate, the payments (or amortization period), the term and any additional clauses to be inserted, like open privileges, assumability and post-dated cheques. Only clauses specified in the offer are picked up in the mortgage.

Buyers who can arrange a VTB fully open mortgage should take full advantage of the maximum flexibility this provides. If a buyer is uncertain of exactly how large a mortgage will be needed for closing, he should opt for the largest possible amount in the offer. If a smaller mortgage is needed, the VTB mortgage can be reduced to the lesser amount, even before closing, without incurring any penalty. This arrangement is ideal for buyers who buy first and do not know exactly how much money will be available from their sale. It also allows first-time buyers to tailor the amount of the mortgage to their financial resources available on closing.

Why do sellers take back mortgages on their own property? To facilitate the sale of the property, plain and simple. If a buyer has to arrange a mortgage, the offer will probably be made conditional on financing, so there will be a delay before the offer becomes firm. Anxiety time for the seller! To avoid this, the vendor may agree to take back the mortgage on specified terms. Presto! Firm offer! Mortgage arranged! No need to be qualified or approved! No delay! No anxiety!

VTB mortgages are often used as a means of marketing the property. They also allow buyers who are borderline in terms of qualifying for a mortgage to complete the transaction. As a further sweetener, most sellers take back their mortgages at rates from ½ to 1½ percentage points below the market rate for mortgages with comparable terms. Liberal open privileges (usually fully open) are also given, as the seller would love to get his unpaid money returned faster! No wonder VTB mortgages are very popular, and enjoy their greatest success in times of high interest rates!

Two points should be noted. First, some sellers will agree to take back the mortgage in the offer, but turn around and immediately sell it through a mortgage broker. This is perfectly legal and does not affect the terms of the mortgage, which are etched in stone in the offer. Although the cheques may be drawn in favor of a different person, everything else stays the same.

Second, sellers holding VTB mortgages may not wish to renew it at maturity. Having financed the purchase for a specified time, sellers are now anxious to have their unpaid money returned. As lenders are under no obligation to renew a mortgage, unless the contract specifically provides, home buyers should be aware that the savings of today may be lost in the future when a new mortgage must be arranged to retire the VTB mortgage.

III.   Buyers of New Homes
Most builders of new homes allow buyers to take over (assume) on closing a mortgage previously negotiated by the builder. Although a financial institution, and not the builder, lends the money and holds the mortgage, most people call this a "builder's mortgage" because its terms are arranged by the builder. Interest rates slightly below current rates may be offered to induce buyers to purchase a newly built home.

It is essential that buyers who will be assuming builders' mortgages take a copy of the offer to their lawyer *before* signing it! Typically, the offer contains many hidden financing clauses buried in its midst. Some of these include allowing the builder/seller to arbitrarily change the interest rate if the quoted mortgage cannot be obtained. Others allow builders to cancel offers in this situation. Many hidden financing costs need be paid, most of which come as a total surprise to most buyers and a shock to their cash flow on closing.

Remember, too, that a very short time is given to apply for a mortgage approval — usually less than one month — even if closing is months away.

8

What Does It Cost To Arrange A Mortgage?

Home buyers are flabbergasted when they learn of the costs incurred in arranging a new loan. Home owners refinancing their existing mortgage are even more dumbfounded — all they are doing is borrowing from Peter to pay Paul, and yet they must absorb such high closing charges.

Whether it be on a purchase or on a refinancing, have a reasonable estimate for *all* of these "hidden costs" provided before signing any mortgage commitment, and plan accordingly. Do not simply ask a lawyer or notary what his fees will be for processing the transaction; legal fees are only one of the many charges incurred when arranging a mortgage. When borrowers are educated and inquisitive, there should be no "hidden costs" on closing. All charges to be paid will be known well ahead of time, eliminating the likelihood of last-minute surprises.

If reasonable estimates of these expenses are not disclosed until shortly before closing, borrowers may have to scramble for more money at the eleventh hour to cover these unexpected costs. Asking the right questions and seeking thorough answers is to the borrower's benefit. Bear in mind as well, as harsh as it sounds, that borrowers pay *all* the costs incurred in processing the transaction, including the lender's costs. Booking and discharging mortgages do not cost lenders anything!

Closing costs are "cash" costs, payable on or before the closing of the transaction. For this reason, borrowers must know *early* about all these costs, if only to avoid a financial crisis at closing. A list of the costs that might be incurred on arranging a new mortgage when purchasing a property or when refinancing an existing loan include the following. Whether any particular item is chargeable depends on the circumstances of the individual loan:

1) Mortgage appraisal/mortgage application fee (see chapter 5).
2) Deduction by the lender for interest to the interest adjustment date. This is a timing problem (see chapter 9).
3) Contribution to establish a realty tax account with the lender (see chapter 10).
4) Mortgage broker's fee (see chapter 7).
5) MICC/CMHC insurance fee, to ensure payments are made on time (see chapter 33).
6) Mortgage insurance fees: fire, life, rate (see chapters 32 and 33).
7) The cost of having a new survey prepared if the existing survey does not reflect current conditions for the property, or if it otherwise is not acceptable to the lender. A common reason is because it is too old.
8) Discharge fees. When an existing loan is refinanced by borrowing from one lender to pay off another, the existing lender will provide the required discharge, upon payment of its discharge fee, usually $100 or more.
9) Prepayment penalty.

10) Legal fees. These could be as high as 1% of the principal amount of the mortgage on a refinancing. In a purchase/mortgage situation, lawyers do levy an extra fee in addition to that charged for the purchase transaction. The additional fee is usually less than that charged for the purchase portion. With much of the work from the purchase transaction being duplicated when processing the mortgage, a reduced charge for the mortgage component is only appropriate.

The services to be performed by a lawyer on a refinancing are virtually the same as when processing a purchase file, so the legal fees on a refinancing are very similar to those charged to home buyers for the purchase component of the transaction. In fact, where mortgages must be paid off and discharged, the fees for the refinancing could exceed those on a purchase. Disbursements are always extra.

Unless valid reasons exist to the contrary, the buyer's lawyer is usually permitted to act for both the purchaser and an institutional lender in a purchase transaction. The same holds true where a new mortgage is being arranged or an existing mortgage is being refinanced — one lawyer represents both borrower and lender, where the lender is a financial institution. Where private funds are being lent, the lender typically will insist on his lawyer acting in the transaction either for both the borrower and the lender, or just for the lender. Having one lawyer represent both sides makes sound financial sense. Involving two law firms, especially in a purchase transaction, means much of the same work is being duplicated. This is an unnecessary expense to the borrower, who ultimately foots the bill for both lawyers.

Although one lawyer is permitted to represent both

borrower and lender in these situations, the arrangement must cease and the lawyer must withdraw completely from acting for either side if a conflict of interest were to arise before the transaction is closed.

In the space below list the reasonable estimates for the costs to be incurred on closing:

1) Mortgage appraisal/mortgage application fee $
2) Deduction by the lender for interest to the interest adjustment date $
3) Contribution to establish a realty tax account with lender $
4) Mortgage broker's fee $
5) MICC/CMHC insurance fee $
6) Mortgage insurance fees $
7) Cost of new survey, if necessary $
8) Discharge fees $
9) Prepayment penalty $
10) Legal fees $_____

    TOTAL $_____

9

Don't Kill That Cash Flow

Timing the closing of a refinancing is very important, because an error could totally destroy the best laid plans of men and mortgagors. Buyers of new and existing houses who grant mortgage loans on closing should also be prepared for unexpected demands on their cash flow, depending on the time of the month when closing takes place.

Most institutional lenders require that mortgage payments be made on the first of each month. As the mortgage is paid "not in advance," the mortgage effectively begins to run starting the first of the month after closing. The first payment is due one month after that date. Not all mortgage transactions close on the first of the month. As a result, the date the mortgage transaction closes has a profound impact on a borrower's cash flow situation.

Sam and Roz bought a house, scheduled to close August 18. The two-year mortgage at the bank at 12½% requires that payments be made the first of the month. The day the mortgage effectively begins to run is the first of the month following closing, in other words September 1. This date is known as the "interest adjustment date." The first payment will be one month after that, namely October 1, covering the interest due for the month of September. The mortgage will mature September 1 two years later.

Interest is still owing to the lender for the "broken period" of August 18 to September 1 because the borrower will have the use of the money during that period of time. Most lenders will deduct from the mortgage advance the interest owing for the 14-day period from August 18 to September 1, calculating the interest daily. On a $50,000 loan, this deduction would be $239.73. Occasionally a lender will make a full advance, and will bill the borrowers for this interest. If the deduction is made on closing, this charge, called deducting interest to the interest adjustment date or IAD, puts a crimp into a borrower's cash flow.

The problem is heightened on a refinancing, where borrowers have two masters to serve — the old and the new lender. Assume Len and Gail refinanced their property like Sam and Roz, on August 18th. The interest adjustment date on Len and Gail's new loan would be September 1. The last payment on their old mortgage would have been made on August 1. The first payment on their new loan is October 1.

The old lender would want, and is entitled to, interest on this mortgage for the additional 17 days in August until the loan is retired. Assuming the rate on that loan was also 12½%, he will be entitled to interest of $278.45. This amount should be calculated semi-annually not in advance, as stated in the mortgage, but often it is calculated monthly when a month is broken. When Len and Gail's financing takes place on August 18, they must pay the old lender the money due to him for the period from August 1 to August 18, *and* the new lender will charge them the interest for the period from August 18 to the interest adjustment date of September

1. The cash flow problem arises because the mortgage payment that would have been made on September 1 for the month of August, in effect, is being made on August 18.

Whether the mortgage is being arranged as part of a purchase or on a refinancing, closing even earlier in the month (i.e., August 8) would compound the problem further. For purchasers, the interest for the broken month otherwise due on September 1 is being deducted "off the top" on August 8. For existing home owners, the mortgage payment for the entire month of August that otherwise would have been due on September 1 is being made on August 8, almost a full month ahead of time.

As in most situations, some rationalization is possible. Although a cash flow crisis may be faced on closing, the saving grace to the transaction is the fact that no mortgage payment in either case will have to be made on September 1. The first payment on the new loan in either case is due on October 1 for the month of September. As nice as it sounds, though, it offers no consolation to the purchaser or home owner whose funds are tight on closing.

If the first payment is exactly one month after the mortgage transaction closes, no cash flow problem exists. Here, the interest adjustment date coincides with the date of closing. Bob and Pauline refinanced their property like Sam and Roz on August 18, with an interest adjustment date of August 18. The first payment will be September 18. No deduction of interest to the IAD is necessary, as the interest adjustment date is the date of closing. Most mortgages with private lenders, especially vendor-take-back mortgages, are written this way.

Consumers who are concerned about this potential cash flow problem can do two things to minimize its effect. One, see if the new lender will bill you for the interest to the interest adjustment date rather than collect it on closing by deducting it from the mortgage proceeds. If this is the case, *get it in writing*! Two, select a closing date for the new mortgage as close to its interest adjustment date as possible, to minimize the amount that could be deducted for this reason.

10

Mortgage Clauses

How do mortgage clauses vary from lender to lender? What are the questions to be asked and the answers to be sought when arranging a mortgage, to make sure it is the most suitable loan for the borrower? Remember, there is more to a mortgage than its interest rate. Eight different categories warrant consideration *before* a mortgage is arranged, whether on a purchase or on a refinancing. These are:

1) interest rate
2) frequency of interest calculations
3) term
4) amortization
5) realty tax account
6) increased monthly payments
7) assumability
8) prepayment and the POPS principle — Paying Off the Principal Sooner — see chapter 11.

In addition, the closing charges (chapter 8) and potential cash flow problems (chapter 9) must be investigated and clearly understood before making a commitment on a mortgage.

1) Interest Rate

In recent years, Canadians have been inundated with advertisements for loans placed by lending institutions, and mortgage loans in particular. Most of the ads quote the lenders' rates of interest, and most of the rates are similar. A random comparison of rates for mortgages with similar terms at different financial institutions at any given point in time would prove this.

Knowing how the banking system works, it is easy to see why rates have to be relatively similar. All lending institutions operate on the "matching principle." Funds are obtained from customers at one rate of interest through their savings operations, and loaned to other customers at a higher rate of interest through their loans departments. The difference in the interest rates — the spread — is the profit margin, and can be as high as three percentage points.

To be competitive in this environment, no financial institution can afford to charge too little or too much on its loans. Too high a rate, and the customers will shy away. Too low a rate, and other lenders will follow suit. Fascinating, isn't it, how other financial institutions act after one lender alters its interest rate on mortgages in response to a change in the Bank of Canada rate, which is a guideline to the cost of money in the marketplace.

Don't be deceived by nominal mark-downs either, such as 12.99% instead of 13%. The total savings monthly on a $50,000 loan, amortized over 25 years, is only 35 cents per month. Hardly worth the effort, if the other mortgage terms won't stand up.

When obtaining a quote for a rate, find out how long the lender will guarantee the rate. Sixty days used to be the norm, but 30 days and fewer are not uncommon to-day. A 21-day guarantee period is little consolation to a buyer who has a 90-day period to closing. The home owner whose mortgage matures in three months will be fearful of another round of high interest rates if the rate for the renewal or refinancing will not be fixed until 15 days before maturity. The fact he may be approved for the loan is meaningless until the actual rate is set. For the purposes of this book, unless otherwise noted only fixed-rate mortgages are being considered. Variable-rate mortgages are still available, but are not nearly as popular as they were several years ago, during the hey-day of the interest rollercoaster ride. Variable rate mortgages, or VRMs, are discussed in chapter 28.

In times of falling interest rates, the lender's rate at the time of closing may be lower than the one appearing in its commitment. Not all lenders will reduce the interest rate charged in the circumstances. Before arranging a loan, ask:

1. Will the borrower get the benefit of any reduction in interest rates before closing?
2. If so, what is the latest date when the "final" rate will be set?
3. Will any administrative charge be incurred for revising the mortgage documents to obtain the lower rate?

Whatever the answers may be, *get them in writing*! No one wants to be told one thing, only to be denied it later for lack of written proof. Protect yourself!

Interest rates can and do vary from lender to lender on occasion, so shop around. I am a staunch believer, however, that there is more — *much more* — to a mortgage than its rate. If the quoted rates are substantially the same, then the other factors should be carefully considered when booking a mortgage loan, for these distinguish one lender's product from another's.

2) Frequency of Interest Calculations
Much confusion exists over the frequency of mortgage *payments*, and the frequency of *interest calculations*.

Mortgages traditionally have been paid monthly. In recent years, lenders have begun accepting mortgage payments weekly, bi-weekly or semi-monthly, to the delight and benefit of home buyers. Yet how often the mortgage is paid is only one factor to consider; how frequently the interest is calculated is crucial as well.

The more frequently interest is calculated (or compounded, the terms being interchangeable) on a mortgage, the greater the yield to the lender. Borrowers, therefore, should be aware of how interest is compounded. Lenders like loans where the payment interval and the interest calculation coincide, for example, monthly. Car loans and personal loans are structured this way. To determine the rate of interest to be charged each month when interest is calculated monthly, simply divide the interest rate by 12. Twelve percent per annum calculated monthly has a monthly interest factor of 1%. By being compounded 12 times a year, an effective annual interest rate of 12.6825% is produced. The effective annual interest rate is the rate of interest the lender receives on the loan at the end of the year.

Interest rates calculated monthly are far and away the easiest to understand and to calculate for blended monthly payments. Unfortunately, they also cost the most for borrowers to carry. In the United States, mortgage interest is calculated monthly. For that reason, mortgage amortization tables from the U.S. will not work for "standard" Canadian mortgages, calculated "semi-annually." Never buy an American amortization book for a Canadian mortgage; it's a waste of money.

According to the *Interest Act of Canada*, when blended payments are made, regardless of how often they are made, the interest rate quoted must be specified as being calculated half-yearly (also known as semi-annually) or yearly, not in advance. Borrowers benefit from this requirement, because calculating interest every six months instead of every month will save them money. (Rates calculated annually are seldom encountered.) Interest rates calculated semi-annually are the norm in Canada.

What are the benefits from interest rates calculated semi-annually? A rate of 12% per annum calculated semi-annually means that 6% is collected every six months. Easy, if the payments are made every six months. However, payments can and usually are made more frequently than interest is calculated. When payments are made monthly and interest is calculated semi-annually, a monthly "interest factor" must be determined, to produce 6% after six months. The monthly interest factor must be less than 1%, as that is the interest factor for a loan where the interest is calculated monthly, not semi-annually. The appropriate interest factor, when compounded six times, must produce 6% after six months. The proper monthly interest factor for 12% calculated semi-annually is .975879403.

Compare two $50,000 loans, amortized over 25 years, with interest calculated at different intervals.

	13% calculated monthly	13% calculated semi-annually
Monthly payment	$563.92	$551.20
Total interest cost	$119,170.70	$115,367.92
Difference	Saved monthly: $12.72	
	Saved over amortized life of loan: $3,802.78	

While it is not wrong for Canadian lenders to charge interest calculated monthly, they can only do so if the mortgage document states what the semi-annual equivalent rate is. Otherwise, trying to compare the two rates is like trying to compare apples and oranges, rather than apples and apples. For example:

13% calculated monthly is equivalent to 13.357% calculated semi-annually
13% calculated semi-annually is equivalent to 13.000% calculated semi-annually
Result: Semi-annual calculations obviously save borrowers money.

Interest rates calculated monthly are encountered most often with second mortgage loans and loans with finance companies and credit unions. Some first mortgages are also calculated monthly. Where interest is calculated monthly, the "semi-annual" equivalent for the interest rate must appear in the mortgage to comply with the *Interest Act of Canada*. *Remember: To save money, be sure the rate quoted is calculated semi-annually and not monthly for a blended payment.*

What does the expression "Not in Advance" mean? Having interest calculated and paid at the end of the period rather than at the start is another important difference between Canadian and American mortgages, a difference which again benefits borrowers. The easiest way to understand the concept is to look at a tenant, Ted. When Ted pays his rent on the first of the month, say January 1, he is doing so in advance for the month to come, the month of January. The landlord gets the use of the money for the entire month. Fred, the home owner, pays his mortgage payment not in advance. The payment for the month of January is not made on January 1; rather, it is made on February 1 ("not in advance"). As a result, Fred, the borrower, has the use of the money for the month of January, and makes his payment on February 1 for the month that has gone by, not the month to come. Because Canadian mortgages are generally payable not in advance, the borrower should ensure that payments on the rate quoted are collected not in advance.

3) Term

Predicting where interest rates will be going in the future means playing the biggest crap game in town! Although selecting the appropriate term for a mortgage, or a mortgage renewal, is not much easier, certain rules should be kept in mind.

Longer-term mortgages bear a higher rate of interest. This is the premium paid for the extended period of security and stability. A 13% mortgage, amortized over 25 years and having a term of three years, will cost Diane and Wayne $551.20 monthly. At the end of the three-year term, $48,971.01 will still be outstanding on the loan. If Lorne and Marlene want security and piece of mind, they might opt for a five-year mortgage at 14%. The 1% differential must be paid *each month* by Lorne and Marlene during the entire term of the mortgage — the first three years as well as the last two years. The payments on their loan are $586.94, and the balance outstanding after three years will be $49,120.12. Regardless of what the interest rates might be at the end of three years, the shorter-term mortgage with the lower interest rate will save Diane and Wayne $35.74 each month for 36 months, or $1,286.64 in payments over the three years (excluding interest on that money). It also means they will owe $149.11 less principal at the end of the three-year term.

This example, however, is not meant to encourage home owners to take the shortest term possible (i.e., cheapest mortgage available). It is meant to show how careful thought is needed in tailoring the mortgage loan to the borrower's needs and circumstances, rather than accepting what is offered "as is." Factors other than just rate must be considered in setting the mortgage term, be it on a home purchase or a refinancing. Families should consider the length of time they expect to remain in the property. Buyers of starter homes or families on the grow may not intend to stay in the property for more than three or four years. If this is the case, then they should choose a mortgage term that reflects this — that corresponds with the anticipated period of ownership. Home buyers who arrange five-year loans will pay more every month for a benefit they will not use. They also could incur a sizeable penalty to prepay the mortgage on the sale of the house before the maturity of the mortgage term, if the mortgage is not fully open. Home buyers should never assume that anyone else will want to take over the mortgage.

During periods of low interest rates, borrowers are encouraged to arrange mortgages for the longest possible term, especially if the loan has full or limited assumption privileges. This should only be done after borrowers have carefully analyzed their own situation first. There is no assurance that any subsequent purchaser of Lorne and Marlene's property will want to assume their mortgage. The outstanding principal could be too small, or it could be too large. A company or family loan might be available at a preferred rate of interest. The purchaser may wish to pay in cash.

If that is the case, then Lorne and Marlene will have to pay a penalty for early termination of the mortgage. They would have been better off, like Diane and Wayne, with a shorter-term mortgage at a lower interest rate.

If in doubt about the maximum term to arrange, stand back and take stock. Consider how long the house can continue to service your needs and wants. If still in doubt, round down the term, not up, to avoid the possibility of a prepayment penalty. The cost of rounding up the mortgage term could prove expensive.

4)   Amortization

Do you remember the four components of a mortgage? Principal, interest rate, amortization period and payments. Remember how changing one factor would change another, if the other two factors remained constant? Shorter amortizations may mean higher payments, but they result in an accelerated reduction of the mortgage loan — POPS. Most of the schemes which are about to be discussed are designed to reduce the amortization on a mortgage in order to reduce the overall interest costs. These ideas apply equally to the home buyer arranging a new mortgage as to a home owner renewing or refinancing an existing mortgage.

The traditional and conventional mortgage amortization has been 25 years, a generation. Just because this was and is the norm, does not mean that it is etched in stone. Shorter amortizations greatly benefit borrowers and should be sought wherever possible. No valid reason exists as to why borrowers who can handle loans with shorter amortizations and who want a reduced amortization period should be denied this arrangement. Still, be prepared for some possible resistance. After all, what is being asked for is somewhat unconventional. Be persistent! All money saved is the borrower's — not the lender's!

What a mortgage really costs to carry is determined to a large extent by the amortization period for the loan.

A reduced amortization is an effective method of reducing the total interest *cost* for the loan, without varying the interest rate. In the following examples, the principal is $50,000 and the interest rate is stated.

12%	25-yr am	20-yr am	15-yr am	10-yr am
Payment	$515.95	$540.49	$590.80	$709.01
Total interest cost	$104,784.59	$79,714.77	$56,346.35	$35,081.98

13%				
Payment	$551.20	$573.77	$621.52	$736.60
Total interest cost	$115,367.71	$87,699.55	$61,872.88	$38,391.53

14%				
Payment	$586.94	$607.59	$652.76	$764.60
Total interest cost	$126,077.56	$95,819.07	$67,499.64	$41,752.06

As the chart indicates, reducing the amortization from 25 to 20 years will cost the borrower under one dollar a day — cigarette money! What a wonderful idea! Stop smoking, and put the money towards a 20-year amortization. Be healthier, save over $25,000 and have five years' fewer mortgage payments to make. That's five years to really enjoy the house, from a health as well as a financial point of view.

Stay away from amortizations of more than 25 years. At one time, longer amortizations of 30 and 35 years were in vogue, especially with rising interest rates, to qualify borrowers for loans under some government programs. As the chart below shows, the savings in monthly payments is more than lost when the total interst cost is considered. Coupled with the fact the loan remains outstanding for another five years, longer amortizations can be harmful to a borrower's financial health.

30-year am	12%	13%	14%
Monthly payment	$503.19	$539.89	$576.97
Savings per month over 25-year am	$12.76	$11.31	$9.97
Total interest cost	$131,160.54	$144,377.42	$157,708.99
Additional cost over 25-year am	$ 26,375.95	$ 29,009.71	$ 31.631.43

When selecting an amortization, the shorter the better. And do a good tailoring job on the payment as well, so it fits the borrower as if it was made to order. Round up the payment as well, to bring interest costs down (see chapter 17).

5) Realty Tax Account
This is the one area that quite aggravates home buyers and home owners. Unpaid property taxes are a special lien against a property, ranking even higher than a first mortgage. To ensure that they retain their first-ranking status at all times, many lenders will collect one-twelfth of the estimated annual realty taxes from the borrower each month, and pay them directly to the municipality. This amount is subject to annual revisions, based on any increase in taxes.

Realty tax accounts can absolutely devastate a buyer's or home owner's cash flow. Depending on the time of year when the transaction closes, three types of realty tax payments may be required: a) the balance of the current year's taxes (this brings the account up-to-date as of December 31); b) an "initial contribution" to establish a tax account (Yes, since all the current year's taxes have been paid, it means that by making an initial contribution a portion of next year's taxes is being paid now. This sum is usually deducted from the mortgage advance, to ensure it is paid.); c) the first monthly payment will include a tax component, representing a portion of next year's taxes as well.

Lenders like to have sufficient funds on hand to honor the tax bills as they are issued. Since tax bills are issued on an interim and final basis, a tax account could have on deposit at the end of one year as much as one-half of *next* year's realty taxes.

When a mortgage is to be discharged, any credit balance in the tax account is used to reduce the amount of the principal owing. Any debit balance is added to increase the amount of the money owing to the lender. Since most tax accounts are maintained in a credit balance, this is a small "saving grace" to borrowers when retiring their loans.

The borrower should also determine whether any interest is paid on the balance in the tax account, and if so, at what rate. Not all lenders pay interest on these accounts, and those who do credit interest at different rates — the savings account rate, an arbitrarily low rate, or the mortgage rate.

If borrowers have at least 50% equity in their property, some lenders will suspend the requirement of a tax account, provided receipted tax bills are delivered annually to the lender. The lender also would reserve the right to enforce the requirement of a realty tax account if realty taxes were unpaid. These arrangements must be made *before* the loan is approved, not afterwards.

If possible, borrowers should try to pay their own taxes. Literally, it is money in the bank, earning interest for the borrower!

6) Increased Payments

This is a relatively new development in Canadian mortgage financing. Will the lender allow an increase in the monthly payment during the term of the mortgage? If a "stepped up" payment is permitted, determine how large an increase is permitted (typically up to 10 or 15% annually), when it can take effect, and whether any administrative costs will be incurred in restructuring the amount of the monthly instalment. The benefits of increased payments are discussed in chapter 19.

7) Assumability

This question, "Is the mortgage assumable if the property is sold?" is often wrongly framed, "Is the mortgage transferable?" In other words, can the mortgage be taken over by a subsequent purchaser of the property? Since the lender holds the mortgage, and the borrower assumes responsibility for the mortgage debt, the question involves assumability, not transferability.

Until the mid-1970s, most mortgages said nothing about their assumability. By being silent on the point, mortgages by law were fully assumable, and that is still the case today. Unless the mortgage specifically says something to the contrary, any buyer could assume any mortgage without having to qualify for the loan, and without requiring the lender's consent to do so.

With the sharp rise in interest rates in the late 1970s and early 1980s, lenders began to demand some say in the matter by inserting different types of "assumability clauses" in the mortgage document.

Three different type of "assumable clauses" now exist.

Fully Assumable: The same situation as before. If there is nothing to the contrary in the mortgage, any buyer of the property can assume it automatically, without having to go through any approval process.

Fully Non-Assumable: The mortgage contains a clause making the mortgage due and payable in full on the sale of the property. No buyer of the property can assume the mortgage. Of course, a lender can waive this clause, but little faith should be placed in that. Known as a "due-on-sale" clause in the United States, its validity has been upheld in provincial Supreme Courts as well as the Supreme Court of the United States.

Limited Assumability or "Due-on-Sale at the Lender's Option": Far and away, this is the most common type of assumable clause. When the property is sold, the lender has the option of either allowing the buyer to assume the mortgage, or requiring the borrower/seller to pay off the loan in full. Usually a lender must be provided with the same information as if the buyer was applying for a new mortgage, and a credit check is conducted.

Before arranging a mortgage with this type of clause, borrowers should learn whether the lender is required to act reasonably in deciding whether to grant his consent. Otherwise, lenders could be both unreasonable and arbitrary in preventing a buyer from assuming the mortgage, despite his financial qualifications. This situation arose in the early 1980s, and could occur again, where the rate on an existing mortgage is low and current interest rates are high. By automatically "calling" all mortgages on properties that are sold, lenders could put the funds back out on the street and get a higher current rate of return. A reasonableness requirement would counteract the potential for heavy-handedness, especially if the buyer otherwise qualifies for the mortgage.

Where the seller takes back the mortgage in the offer, rarely is a clause inserted limiting its assumability. Most VTB mortgages, therefore, are automatically and totally assumable by subsequent buyers of the property.

Obviously, borrowers prefer fully assumable loans. When interest rates are high, a fully assumable mortgage at a rate of interest below current rates is marketed as a prominent selling feature of a house, like lot size and area of the dwelling. If a fully assumable loan cannot be arranged, the buyer should insist on a limited assumability clause containing a reasonable requirement as a bare minimum.

Whenever a mortgage is assumed by a new buyer, the original borrower is not automatically off the hook, to the surprise and chagrin of many borrowers. The mortgage, after all, is a contract, and the borrower's liability remains in effect throughout the term of the contract. In Ontario, as in most provinces, the lender can recover the amount outstanding on a defaulted mortgage from either the original borrower or the then owner of the property, but not from both. Most lenders will proceed against the current owner of the property, but they need not do so, especially if land values have fallen dramatically since the mortgage was arranged, thereby eroding the current owner's equity. Only when the mortgage has matured is the original borrower's liability fully at an end.

How are mortgages "assumed"? In most resale transactions, after being approved by the lender, if required, the buyer closes the deal. That's it. By closing the transaction, registering the deed and making future mortgage payments, the buyer has implied he will assume the mortgage through his actions.

New home transactions are treated differently; buyers are required to sign a formal mortgage assumption agreement, making a direct contractual link between the buyer and the lender which otherwise would not exist. The agreement often takes the form of a mortgage assumption and amending agreement, in which buyer and lender agree to vary some of the terms of the mortgage, as registered on title. A need for such an agreement would arise if the buyer assumed a smaller principal than is registered on title, if the payments or interest rate were changed, or if the payment dates were altered. Recently, some lenders have begun using these agreements even in resale transactions, especially where the lender's prepayment privileges have been broadened over time.

11

Prepaying The Mortgage With The POPS Principle

Prepaying a mortgage is a different kettle of fish than *repaying* a mortgage. The same blended amount paid month after month is the amount *repaid* to the lender. Extra money given to the lender by the borrower during the term of the mortgage constitutes the *prepayment* — paid before its time. Both home buyers and home owners alike must be familiar with the rules of the prepayment game in order to know what questions to ask, and what answers to seek in choosing the best "tailor made" prepayment option available. Since not all mortgages are created equal, the different prepayment options could be the deciding factor in choosing one lender over another.

What is POPS?

The albatross for most people about mortgages is the interest cost of the loan, which is often two to three times the amount of the principal originally borrowed. Absolutely astronomical! Anything that will reduce the interest *cost* to a borrower can only help.

The whole idea behind the POPS principle — Paying Off the Principal Sooner — is to return the lender's money to him as soon as possible. A lender arranges a mortgage loan amortized over many years with the assumption that the payments will be made on time, that the loan will be renewed punctually, and that the loan will be outstanding for the entire amortized period. Any *additional* amount paid to the lender before it is due is applied directly to the outstanding principal. Every dollar prepaid by a borrower to his lender not only accelerates the reduction of the outstanding principal, but also reduces the period of time needed to retire the loan in full. Returning the lender's money faster reduces the amortization for the loan, and results in large interest savings for the borrower.

Prepaying or POPS is one of the easiest and most beneficial ways of dealing with the high cost of mortgage financing, and is the most powerful way of increasing home equity quickly.

Why take advantage of POPS?

What is the primary reason for playing the POPS game? It is to reduce the high interest costs associated with home ownership. Remember, residential mortgage interest payments in Canada, unlike the United States, generally are not deductible from other income. Therefore, mortgages in Canada are paid with after-tax dollars, funds on which income tax has already been paid. Obviously, the amount of before-tax dollars needed to finance a mortgage is even higher.

Learning the amount of income that must be earned to finance a mortgage in Canada is disheartening to most people. The $50,000 mortgage at 13% referred to earlier would require a total repayment of principal and interest of $165,367.71 over its 25-year amortized life. Being in the 30% marginal tax bracket (discussed below), Denis and Marie must earn $236,239.89 *before* taxes to finance this mortgage. Gary and Barb, who are in the 35% marginal tax bracket, have to earn $254,412.18 *before* taxes to carry this mortgage over its amortized life. The "true cost" of carrying a mortgage is absolutely staggering.

In Canada, the *Income Tax Act* permits the first $1,000 of investment income to be earned tax free. Since spouses easily can double-up on this exemption, full advantage should be made of this provision first. Once the full exemption has been used, the next step in applying the POPS principle is for borrowers — both home owners and home buyers — to calculate their marginal tax rate. This is the rate of tax charged by the government on the last dollar of income earned. It can be located on Schedule 1 of an income tax return. Remember to consider the rate of tax charged by *both* the federal and provincial governments. The marginal tax rate helps to determine whether putting POPS to work is a sound economic decision by indicating what before-tax rate of return must be earned on comparable alternative investments.

Joe and Kay's mortgage is at 12%, and their marginal tax rate is 33½%. The formula to calculate the before-tax rate of interest that must be earned, comparable to a 12% investment by way of prepayment, is:

$$\frac{\text{Mortgage Rate}}{(1 \text{ less Marginal Tax Rate})} = \frac{12}{.66666} = 18\%$$

If the alternative investment did not earn 18% before tax, utilizing POPS makes more financial sense. For Charlie and Diana, whose mortgage rate is 13½% and whose marginal tax rate is 40%, their alternative investment must be 22½% to be economically worthwhile.

Paying Off Principal Sooner really means investing in oneself and in one's own home. Owing less money on a home brings substantial peace of mind to many home owners. It means that the magic day when the property is owned "free and clear" is ever closer. When asked why they would prepay a mortgage with a 5% interest rate with three years to run, home owners reply in unison, "Now, nobody can take my house away!"

Home owners whose mortgages matured during periods of high interest rates benefited if they owed as little as possible on their mortgage, through making prepayments. They were able to renew or refinance the loan with lower monthly payments. The same would obviously hold true if borrowers were to face another round of high interest rates in the future.

Since mortgages are front-end loaded — the highest interest charges being in the earliest years of the loan — any scheme that will get more money paid towards principal early in the amortized life of the loan will substantially reduce its amortization period. This in turn will have a dramatic effect in reducing the overall interest costs of the loan. The extra money paid towards principal could be a lump-sum payment, a regularized increase in monthly payment, faster payments (weekly) or through the application of any of the prepayment ideas mentioned in this book. This is the greatest benefit for making use of POPS — and is equivalent to earning the marginal tax rate on the amount prepaid.

A secondary benefit is the shift in the allocation of the blended payment between principal and interest. Once a prepayment is made, a larger portion of each subsequent payment will be allocated to principal than would otherwise have been the case. With more of the payment going towards principal in the future, savings are compounded as well.

The principle is clear: POPS — Paying Off the Principal Sooner — is the name of the game. Take advantage of it to the fullest extent possible.

What are the disadvantages of POPS?

While sinking money into one's own property is not really the same as sinking money down a dry hole, there is one striking similarity. It is very difficult to get the money back. Prepaying a mortgage is not a liquid form of an investment, like a bank account or Canada Savings Bonds. (A liquid investment is one where the funds can be obtained almost immediately at little or no expense.) The money invested into the house remains part of borrower's increased equity, and is not available unless the property is sold or the amount of the mortgage is increased — a costly and time-consuming procedure.

The reduction in the buying power of the dollar in times of inflation is another drawback to prepaying a mortgage. Every month, Statistics Canada tells the public how the cost of living has increased, and how a dollar worth 100 cents in 1971 may only be worth two-thirds of that today. Borrowing money in 1985 and repaying it in later years benefits home buyers, the argument goes, because the money that is paid back is worth less than the money that was borrowed. It is better not to pay additional money towards the house, the argument continues, to maximize the effects of inflation.

As cogent as these arguments might be from an economic point of view, they have not swayed borrowers. The tangible benefits of being able to burn the mortgage, not having to make monthly payments to a lender and not getting caught in an interest rate squeeze motivate most borrowers to prepay loans as quickly as they can. While belt-tightening may be needed for a few years, most borrowers look forward to the not-too-distant future when they can "live and breathe" without a mortgage.

The effect of inflation on mortgages has been somewhat overstated as well. Mortgages are extremely top-heavy in terms of interest in their early years. Most of the interest must be paid at a time when a dollar has much the same value as when it was borrowed. Shaving down interest costs means enormous savings to borrowers today, in today's dollars, and not in devalued and depreciated dollars of the future.

As with any other form of investment, one's individual circumstances and financial condition must be carefully analyzed before putting any additional funds towards the mortgage. Borrowers should only proceed if they are confident that the funds prepaid will not be needed for other purposes in the foreseeable future. In any event, under no circumstances should borrowers prepay their mortgages without leaving a reserve of liquid funds for an emergency. To do so could result in being asset rich but cash flow poor.

The next few chapters explain the POPS principle in greater detail.

12

How Open Is Open?
The Full Story On
Prepayment Privileges

A mortgage that allows a measure of prepayment in addition to the regular monthly payment is considered to have "open" privileges. To many people "open," therefore, is synonymous with the right to prepay the mortgage. Unfortunately, much confusion has arisen over the concept of "open", because different degrees of "openness" exist from lender to lender. *Just because a mortgage is said to be "Open" does not necessarily mean that it is "Fully Open" and that the entire amount can be prepaid at any time without penalty.* When shopping for a mortgage, either to finance a purchase or to refinance an existing loan, it is absolutely essential to find out whether the mortgage is open, and if so, to what extent. No one wishing to bring the POPS principle into play wants to learn that, at the time the prepayment is to be made, the privilege is more restricted than anticipated.

The competition for mortgage business has heated up considerably in the past few years. While prepayment privileges offered by the country's leading financial institutions may appear both restrictive and diverse (standardization being sorely needed), they are considerably more liberal than was the case just a few short years ago.

By law, all mortgages are closed, with no right to prepay the mortgage, unless the mortgage specifically contains a right to prepay the mortgage. In one limited situation, the right to prepay is also given by statute (discussed below). Although they are not obligated to do so, most financial institutions gratuitously include clauses in their mortgages permitting borrowers to pre-pay some money at some time on some terms during the life of the mortgage. So many prepayment variations exist in the marketplace, however, that they literally are all over the map.

Prepayments can be made in three different forms: 1) a lump-sum amount paid to the lender, discussed in this chapter. This is the most common type of pre-payment privilege; 2) a fixed increase in the monthly payment (see chapter 19); and 3) an increase in the fre-quency of mortgage payments through weekly, bi-weekly and semi-monthly payments (see chapter 25).

Five different categories of lump-sum prepayment clauses exist, with variations within each category. Be careful. Some loans fit into one category for part of the term, but into another for the balance of the loan.

A)   Fully Open: No Notice or Penalty — This is the most beneficial privilege for borrowers who wish to employ POPS. The entire principal, or any part of it, can be prepaid at any time without giving any prior notice to the lender and without having to pay any penalty or bonus interest. Borrowers often pay a premium of one-half percent or more for this type of privilege.

B) Open with a Fixed Penalty or Notice —
Similar to category **A** in that the entire principal or any
part of it can be prepaid. To do so, a specific penalty,
which is clearly spelled out in the mortgage, must be
paid, or the appropriate amount of notice must be given
when prepaying the mortgage. Generally, the penalty
charged is three months' interest on the amount prepaid.
For this reason it is open in a qualified manner, but not
fully open. The amount of the penalty exacted or the
notice period required do differ from lender to lender.

This category has become increasingly popular in recent years. Many lenders' prepayment privileges follow
category **C** for part of the term of the mortgage, and
then shift into this category for the remainder of the
term. For example, a 10% prepayment privilege might
exist for the first two years of a three-year mortgage,
while in the third year the loan is open on payment of a
three months' interest penalty.

**C) Limited Open Privilege: No Penalty or
Notice —** This type of mortgage is open to a limited
extent (i.e., 10% annually) without any notice and
without payment of any penalty. The remainder of the
mortgage is closed. Just because the loan has limited
prepayment privileges does not mean it is a 100% open
mortgage. Unfortunately for borrowers, the mortgage is
silent about the penalty or notice required to prepay the
closed portion of the mortgage — the remaining 90%.
This has been the most common type of mortgage
available, and still is quite common, although some
loans shift into category **B** after a specified period of
time.

D)   Limited Open Privilege: Fixed Penalty or Notice — This mortgage is a hybrid of the second and third categories. Like the third type, a limited open prepayment privilege exists in the mortgage (i.e., 10% annually), while the rest of the mortgage is closed. Like the second type, a specified interest penalty must be paid or a fixed amount of notice must be given by the borrower to utilize the prepayment privilege. Like the third type, although it may be open with restrictions to a certain extent, the remainder of the loan (90%) is closed.

E)   Fully Closed — No automatic right to prepay any portion of the principal exists at any time during the term of the mortgage. Only the regular monthly payments can be made — nothing more.

NOTE THAT ALL MORTGAGES, OF WHATEVER CATEGORY, ARE FULLY OPEN ON THEIR MATURITY!

Within each category, other factors determine how much can be prepaid and when. These vary greatly from lender to lender, and are responsible for the myriad of possibilities that borrowers face in selecting both the mortgage and the mortgagee lender. These "distinguishing factors" include:

How generous is the prepayment privilege?
For limited prepayment privilege mortgages, the degree of openness depends on the individual lender. Some permit a maximum annual prepayment of 5%, others 10%, and others 15%. Most (but not all) lenders base this on the amount of the original amount borrowed, rather than the amount outstanding. This means the same maximum can be prepaid each time.

Is the prepayment privilege cumulative or noncumulative?

Most limited prepayment clauses set a maximum prepayment percentage which is noncumulative. Using a 10% annual prepayment privilege on a $60,000 mortgage as an example, if only $4,000 is prepaid the first year the clause is used, the unused portion is lost forever. It cannot be added to the privilege that may be used in a subsequent year, to permit a prepayment of more than $6,000.

Is there a minimum that must be prepaid?

To avoid having to process small prepayments, some lenders set a minimum amount that must be paid to invoke the clause. The amount varies from lender to lender, from $100 to $500 and even $1,000.

Must a prepayment be made in accordance with the amortization schedule?

To avoid having to order a new amortization schedule each time a prepayment is made, some lenders require that the amortization schedule for the loan be followed when a prepayment is made. This means the prepayment can only be made on a regular payment date, and at no other time during the month. How to prepay in accordance with an amortization schedule is described in chapter 16.

The timing of a prepayment:

Not too long ago, one prepayment was permitted each mortgage year, on the interest adjustment date of the mortgage. George and Rochelle's three-year mortgage was booked on May 20, 1985, with an interest adjustment commencing June 1. The only days the mortgage could be prepaid are June 1, 1986, or June 1, 1987. On

June 1, 1988, the mortgage becomes fully open. If they are unable to prepay on those dates, the prepayment privilege will be nullified. For example, if they want to prepay the mortgage on any day other than June 1 of each year, the prepayment privilege will be useless.

In recent years, the times when prepayments can be made have been liberalized by lenders. No longer are borrowers restricted by some lenders to just one prepayment opportunity each mortgage year, on only one specific date. (The first mortgage year would run from June 1, 1985 to May 31, 1986.) Instead, these borrowers can exercise their prepayment privilege once each mortgage year *on any of the 12 regular payment dates (i.e., the first of the month).* This means that George and Rochelle still can prepay their mortgage only once each mortgage year, yet the number of opportunities to do so within that mortgage year has increased 12 times.

Some lenders now even permit prepayments to be made once each *calendar* year, on any regular payment date. This gives borrowers one extra opportunity to prepay their loan. If their mortgage was for three years with an interest adjustment date of June 1, 1985, George and Rochelle could prepay their mortgage once in 1985, once in 1986, once in 1987 and once in 1988. Of course, any prepayment must be made on a regular payment date. In addition, the mortgage can also be prepaid in full on its maturity.

Fully open loans, on the other hand, have become more restrictive in recent years. Originally, a prepayment could be made at any time; on a payment date, mid-month, or even the day before the payment date. While lenders recovered interest to the actual date of payment, it led to much confusion when prepayments were made in mid-month. Now, many lenders' fully open clauses restrict prepayments to the payment date only. In turn, prepayment in accordance with the amortization schedule is encouraged, which must be on a payment date to be effective.

When a prepayment has to be made on the interest adjustment date, check the payment dates extremely carefully. With an interest adjustment date of June 1, the first payment would have been on July 1. The right to prepay would not be one year after the date of the first payment, but one year after the interest adjustment date (or 11 months after the first payment). In other words, the right to prepay would fall on June 1. Borrowers wishing to invoke the prepayment privilege have been denied the right in the past because they have incorrectly determined the date when the prepayment privilege could be used.

When does the prepayment privilege start?
Not all mortgages give a prepayment privilege during the first year of the mortgage term. In some long-term mortgages the right only exists after a certain period of time, such as one or two years following the interest adjustment date.

What type of prepayment is allowed?
Does the mortgage permit lump-sum payments only, or are increases in the regular monthly payment also permitted? Most prepayment privileges are restricted to lump-sum payments. Only a handful of lenders permit a direct "step-up" in the regular monthly payment. Unless such a right exists in the mortgage, the regular monthly payment cannot be increased over the term of the mortgage.

If monthly payments are increased, the result is the amortization for the loan must decrease. After one year's payments, on a $50,000 mortgage at 13% amortized over 25 years, the outstanding balance is $49,699.18. If the monthly payment is increased permanently from $551.20 to $600.00 commencing with the first payment in the second year and is never changed after that, the remaining interest cost on the loan would be reduced from $109,054.13 to $68,702.76 — a drop of 37% by increasing the monthly payment only once! Regular increases in mortgage payments are an effective way to reduce the amortization for a loan and to apply the POPS principle.

Borrowers with fully open mortgages should be aware they can prepay their mortgages little by little each month by directly increasing the amount of the regular monthly payment. Even borrowers with limited prepayment privileges can increase their regular monthly payment with an indirect increase in the monthly payment. See chapter 21.

When a borrower wishes to prepay the open portion of a closed mortgage, what is the usual penalty?
In this situation, we are looking at the 10% limited prepayment privilege offered gratuitously by lenders. Many lenders do not charge any penalty if a prepayment is made under this clause, meaning the loan falls into category **C**. If a penalty is charged (the loan falling into category **D**), three months' bonus interest on the amount prepaid is the standard charge. This is a *contractual* term that appears right in the mortgage. It is not a matter for negotiation. The remainder of the mortgage, of course, is closed, no prepayment being permitted.

Three months' bonus interest paid to the lender does not mean that three times the mortgage payment is the penalty. Rather, three times the interest component *only* of the most forthcoming mortgage payment would be the penalty. Fred and Shirley have a five-year, $50,000 mortgage at 13% with a 25-year amortization that allows prepayment up to 10% of the original principal each year. After three years (payment 36), when they still owed $48,971.01, they decided to pay 10% of the outstanding principal, or $4,897.10. Although the monthly payment is $551.20, the penalty should not be three times that amount, or $1,653.60. When calculating the penalty, do not look at the payment, look at the figure for interest; the penalty is based on the interest component only, and not interest plus principal. To pay off the entire principal, the penalty would be $516.70 times three, which is $1,550.10. To pay off 10% of the principal will result in a penalty of $155.01. (See "Amortization Schedule" in Appendix B for principal and interest components.)

Note that where private lenders are involved, the stated penalty for the amount prepaid is often less than three months' interest.

For loans in category **B**, the amount of the penalty that would have to be paid to retire the loan *in full* is also clearly stated right in the mortgage document, and is not a matter of negotiation. Borrowers whose mortgages fall into categories **C**, **D** and **E** are not so fortunate.

When a borrower wishes to pay the closed portion of a closed mortgage, what is the usual penalty?
This is the dilemma that borrowers whose mortgages fall into categories **C**, **D** and **E** face.

Contrary to generally accepted public thinking, *there is no automatic right to pay off any mortgage with a payment of three months' interest penalty.* Anyone who says this is so, is misleading the public. The part of the loan we are concerned about is not the 10% "open" portion of the loan, for that is specifically dealt with in the contract. Rather, it is the 90% or so of the mortgage (or 100% of a fully closed mortgage) which is not specifically covered by the prepayment clause in the mortgage — the "closed" portion of the loan.

When interest rates were stable, the accepted rule of thumb on negotiating the prepayment of the closed portion of the loan (in other words, to break the loan) was a three months' interest penalty on the amount prepaid. Because there is no obligation on a lender's part to permit an early prepayment of the entire mortgage, borrowers have found that high interest rate mortgages cannot be prepaid in this fashion. Since the borrower is asking the lender to break an otherwise enforceable contract, the lender has the power of veto with regard to permitting a premature payment of the loan and, if permitted, can determine what the interest penalty will be.

Borrowers in categories **C, D** and **E** who wish to prepay the closed portion of their mortgages remain at the whim and discretion of their lender. The mortgage is silent about what the prepayment penalty would be for this portion of the mortgage, and the lender holds all the cards.

It is essential to understand the difference between the contractual right to prepay the *open* portion of a closed loan, and the need to negotiate a penalty if a borrower wishes to prepay the *closed* portion of his mortgage. Too many times clients have come to me, attempting to prepay their mortgage, claiming their loan is fully open. On further analysis it is clear the mortgage has a limited open option, perhaps 10%, but that the rest of the mortgage is closed. I explain the 10% open privilege can be used if the contractual criteria are met. Then, regretfully, I must ask what do we do about the other 90% of the loan — the part not spelled out in the contract. This is the real problem.

With the recent instability of the mortgage interest rates, no standard penalty exists any longer to break a mortgage. Penalties as high as six months' interest have been upheld by the courts as being valid. Yet, a development within the past year is now giving borrowers a better idea of what the penalty to prepay a mortgage will be.

What are "present value" prepayments?
An exciting new development in the area of prepaying mortgages is the gradual acceptance and implementation by some institutional lenders of the idea of present value prepayments. *Also known as current value adjustments, the prepayment penalty charged is the present value of the difference in interest rates on the amount being prepaid for the remainder of the mortgage term.* The loan is taken out of categories **C, D** or **E** and is placed in category **B**. If this alternative is presented as the manner in which the prepayment penalty will be calculated, be absolutely sure the *present value* of the interest differential is determined, not just the interest rate differential itself. This distinction is crucial.

Besides the administrative costs involved in early prepayment of a mortgage, it is only fair that lenders be compensated for the interest lost arising from the prepayment. Some lenders were asking borrowers for the full interest rate differential between the current mortgage rates and the contractual mortgage rate for the balance of the mortgage term. Instead of benefiting borrowers, this scheme proved to be a windfall for lenders.

By paying the loss of interest differential "up front" at

the time the mortgage is discharged, lenders were receiving a lump sum now that they otherwise would be receiving little by little over the remainder of the mortgage term. The lender, and not the borrower, would get the interest on this money — therefore the windfall for the lender. In the usual situation, the rate of interest in the mortgage being prepaid is higher than the current interest rates.

Peter and Cathy wish to prepay their five-year $50,000 mortgage at 16% amortized over 25 years. Three years have run on their mortgage. Current interest rates have fallen to 12%. The amount outstanding at this time is $49,360.95. To look strictly at the interest rate differential would mean charging Peter and Cathy 4% of $49,360.95 for two more years, or $3,948.88. This approach does not acknowledge that the money will now be paid by the borrower to the lender, rather than over the next two years, and can be invested to generate further interest for the lender.

The present value approach takes this into account. It recognizes that if the money is prepaid today, the lender will get only 12% and not 16% by putting it back on the street. While lenders should be compensated for their losses, they also will be earning interest at 12% (current rate) on the lump-sum penalty paid, for the remainder of the mortgage term. The penalty, therefore, should be the present value of the difference, for the remaining term of the mortgage, between the payments at the current interest rate and the payments at the contractual mortgage interest rate. Using this formula, which is somewhat complicated to work through, the prepayment penalty would be only $3,295.10.

Some lenders have begun adopting this scheme in a modified form. One bank will charge borrowers as a prepayment penalty a minimum of $500, or the penalty using the present value approach. Another charges the present value prepayment penalty plus an administration fee of $500, which is reduced by $100 in each subsequent year. The move to present value prepayments is on!

It is true that present value prepayments still cost borrowers the contractual mortgage interest rate for the balance of the mortgage term. Instead of paying the higher interest rate on the oustanding principal each month until the mortgage matures, borrowers utilizing present value prepayments are paying the difference in the interest rates now, up-front, rather than little-by-little, over time. More importantly, though, present value prepayments prevent lenders from receiving the interest rate differential as a prepayment penalty — and then receiving interest on that sum as well!

In February, 1984, the Federal Budget proposed that *all* borrowers "should have the right to prepay their mortgages." To open up all mortgages, and to prevent exorbitant penalties, "the maximum amount that lenders can collect is the present value of the loss incurred as a result of the prepayment." Unfortunately, the amendments were not passed before the September 1984 election was called, and therefore are not law at the writing of this book.

In the reverse situation, where current interest rates are higher than the contractual mortgage interest rate, borrowers are still being penalized, even in the application of present value prepayments. While rates fell in Peter and Cathy's situation, Antoine and Joan face the reverse situation. Their mortgage is at 12%, and they need to prepay their loan in full when interest rates have risen to 16% (they have sold their house and the new owner is getting a company loan). What's sauce for the goose should be sauce for the gander! Unfortunately, that's not the case. If lenders can charge a present value penalty when interest rates fall and loans are prepaid, shouldn't borrowers get a rebate if the reverse is true? Should not the present value of the difference, for the remaining term of the mortgage, between the payments at current rates (16%) and the payment of the mortgage interest rate (12%) be paid to Antoine and Joan? After all, the lender can take the outstanding money, currently bearing 12%, and get 16% for it on the street! The Federal Budget did not address this point, and lenders do not want to discuss it either. The principle, though, is equally sound. Maybe someday . . . Nevertheless, even if no rebate is paid to borrowers, no prepayment penalty should be incurred if current interest rates exceed the contractual rate. Any penalty charged defeats the entire purpose of present value prepayments.

If the lender is prepared to negotiate and settle the interest penalty based on interest rate differentials, be absolutely sure they are adjusted to reflect the present value of the differential.

In the space below, determine the terms being offered by various lenders for their mortgages. Analyze them and compare them before making a final decision on the loan.

Terms	Lenders	1	2	3
Loans officer: name and telephone				
What open privileges are there?				
Other factors to note:				
1) how much can be prepaid and what is the penalty?				
2) cumulative/noncumulative				
3) minimum amount to be prepaid				
4) amortization schedule to be followed?				
5) timing of prepayment				
6) when does prepayment start?				
7) lump-sum versus increased payments				
8) are present value prepayments allowed?				

13

Open Mortgages — Where Are You?

Until the late 1960s, mortgage terms and amortizations coincided. The 25-year term/25-year amortization was the industry standard. As interest rates rose, the five-year mortgage came into vogue, amortized over 25 years. That continued until the late 1970s. Today, with the volatility of the interest rate market, short-term mortgages are prevelant. Only a handful of mortgages are booked for terms of more than three years. Since all mortgages are fully open on their maturity, and can be prepaid in full or in part without penalty at that time, the obvious advantage of short-term mortgages is the increased opportunity they present to prepay the loan without penalty when they mature.

Few institutions offer conventional first mortgages that are fully open with no prepayment penalty. Some will grant open mortgages by booking what are called "collateral" mortgages; the money lent to the borrower is considered to be a personal loan, secured initially by a promissory note. As additional or collateral security, the bank or trust company will take a mortgage registered against the borrower's house. Through these legal gymnastics, the financial institution grants a personal loan to the borrower, typically an open type of loan (but check this out ahead of time)! It has not pre-judiced its position, because it still has a first mortgage encumbering the borrower's property for the full amount of the loan. The difference is one of form than of substance.

Borrowers beware, however. As personal loans, collateral mortgages are calculated monthly, meaning a higher interest cost to the borrower. They also can bear interest at least 1% higher than for a conventional mortgage, adding further additional costs to be considered.

Two other sources of open mortgages are private lender and vendor-take-back (VTB) mortgages. Many VTB mortgages are structured as fully open (category **A**), although some do contain an interest penalty (putting the loan into category **B**). Because of the circumstances in which they are arranged, they are typically available at or even below current interest rates.

Mortgages from private individuals may be fully open or they may be open, but have restrictions. The mortgage may be open only after a specified "closed" period, meaning the loan shifts from category **E** to category **A** or **B** after a period of time. Also, a fixed prepayment penalty may have to be incurred to invoke the privilege (category **B**).

More and more financial institutions are adopting a limited application of the open approach, but not without its costs. Following a closed period, with limited prepayment privileges (category **C** or **D**), the mortgage becomes open (category **B**). The penalty to prepay may be three months' bonus interest, the present value of the interest differential, or a combination of the two.

Fully open mortgages are expensive, no doubt about it. Unless the mortgage is a vendor-take-back loan arranged to sell the house, expect to pay a premium upwards of one-half of one percent, maybe even more, for the open privilege. The question then becomes, is it worth the additional cost? Carey and Sharon are debating whether to accept a $50,000 mortgage at 13% with a 10% prepayment privilege, or a fully open loan at 14%. The difference in the monthly payment is $35.74; over a three-year mortgage this privilege will then cost them $1,286.64. While Carey and Sharon would like the security of being able to prepay the loan without any penalty at any time they wished, they consider it an expensive luxury. As they are looking at the house as a three- to five-year investment, there is little likelihood of using the fully open privilege anyway. The gratuitous 10% prepayment privilege more than meets their needs. With a relatively short term, the mortgage will be fully open in three years' time with no penalty.

For long-term mortgages, borrowers are already paying a premium for the long-term commitment. The additional cost of having a fully open mortgage could make the loan impossible to carry. Deciding whether or not to pay the price can only be made after a careful evaluation of the borrower's financial situation, which should be done any time a mortgage loan is booked.

14

How To Benefit From Playing The POPS Game

Interest is rent paid by borrowers for the use of the lender's money. The shorter the time the money is borrowed, the less the borrower has to pay in rent.

Prepaying a mortgage does not change the amount of the regular monthly payment. The miracle of POPS arises as by making a prepayment — by paying additional money towards principal before it is due, no interest will ever have to be paid again to the borrower on the amount prepaid. With mortgages being front-end loaded (the bulk of the interest being paid in the early years of the loan), a prepayment at that time greatly reduces the interest cost for the loan.

Kevin and Sheri borrowed $50,000 at 13% amortized over 25 years. Payments are blended, $551.20 a month. The total interest cost for this mortgage, over its 25-year amortized life, will be $115,367.71. Of course, the $50,000 principal will have to be repaid as well. At the end of the first year of regular payments, they will have paid $6,614.40, but will have only increased their equity by $300.82. The other $6,313.58 is interest, interest and more interest. If Kevin and Sheri paid $500 towards their mortgage at the end of the first year, and never made another prepayment, they would save $9,430.22

in increased costs! Amazing! Even a prepayment of $100 at the end of the first year only would save them $2,026.38 in interest, money that otherwise would have to be paid in after-tax dollars. If anyone knows of an attractive investment with a 2,000% return, please let me know. I would like to become his or her partner!

If $500 was prepaid at the end of the first year, and a further $500 is prepaid at the end of the second, third, fourth and fifth years, a total of $26,916.09 would be saved — over 23% of the total interest cost for the loan. Of course these calculations assume no penalty is incurred on the prepayment.

Convinced? Looking for a way to reduce those after-tax dollar high-interest costs? Borrowers who want to play POPS with their own mortgages need only read on to see how!

15

Get That Amortization Schedule — NOW!

A common complaint about playing the POPS game is, that while all these numbers look nice, the average person cannot really see in black and white what the benefits are for himself. Blended payments are confusing enough; trying to figure out where one stands at any point in time is even harder. If a prepayment is made, the borrower's monthly payment doesn't change, and the money remains with the lender. How can anyone *really* know and be sure that all that interest is being saved? How can the average home owner and home buyer who do not know how to calculate amortization schedules and to whom compound interest theory is a high school subject that has long been forgotten, check all this out?

The key for borrowers playing and benefitting from POPS is having a tailor-made amortization schedule for the mortgage loan. "Am" schedules, as they are called, give a detailed financial analysis of a mortgage. They show the amount of the regular monthly payment, its allocation between principal and interest, and the outstanding balance after each payment is made. Amortization schedules are available at nominal cost (under $10) from a number of computer companies in Canada.

Look in the *Yellow Pages* of a major metropolitan centre under the heading "Mortgage Amortization Schedules."

To order a personalized schedule, the following information is needed; most of it is available from the mortgage document or the lender. If in doubt, verify the information with the lender *before* ordering the amortization schedule:

(a) The outstanding principal after the most recent payment was made. This will be the amount of the loan for new mortgages.   _____

(b) The interest rate   _____

(c) How frequently it is calculated (semi-annually?)   _____

(d) The amount of the payment. Only include the principal and interest component, *not* the tax portion.   _____

(e) How frequently it is paid (i.e., monthly)   _____

(f) Whether the payment is blended (principal and interest), principal plus interest, or interest only   _____

(g) The date of the *next* payment (mortgages are paid in arrears, or technically "not in advance")   _____

To play POPS, it is necessary to order an amortization schedule for the entire amortized life of the loan (i.e., 25 years), even though the mortgage term itself will be considerably shorter. Therefore, order a schedule "to maturity" rather than for a fixed number of years. Armed with an am schedule, borrowers are ready to unlock the door to the mystery and miracle of prepayment.

16

How To Read
An Amortization Schedule

Amortization schedules are very easy documents to read and understand. All it takes is a few minutes to get used to the manner in which the information is presented. Once borrowers become comfortable with its format, understanding what the schedule has to offer readily follows.

First of all, verify the information at the top of the schedule. Little is gained by working with an incorrect schedule. Again, be sure the first payment date is correct. Otherwise, the whole schedule is out of whack. For existing loans, the first payment date is the date of next upcoming payment. For new loans, the first payment date is one month after the interest adjustment date. Also note that the schedule provides the interest factor for the mortgage. For loans calculated semi-annually, this figure should be less than the quoted interest rate divided by 12 (which is the interest factor for loans calculated monthly).

The payment number shows which amortization payment is being made at any given time. The total payment is the total blended monthly amount (principal and interest, *but never including taxes*) that will be paid over the full amortized life of the loan. Although the term will be shorter than the amortization, the monthly payment is needed to show how the next two items are determined, the interest component and the principal component. By obtaining a schedule to maturity, the breakdown of every payment over the amortized life of the loan is shown. Some schedules also provide the total of interest and principal paid each calendar year — of greater relevance to lenders than borrowers.

Look at the Amortization Schedule in Appendix B for the loan that Kevin and Sheri arranged. With a conventional blended mortgage, each payment gradually decreases the amount of principal that is outstanding. The first payment consists of a principal component of $23.65, and an interest component of $527.55. After this payment is made, the outstanding principal is reduced to $49,976.35. Since interest is charged only on the previous month's outstanding balance, slightly more money is allocated to principal than in the previous month, while slightly less money is allocated to interest. Therefore, in the second month the principal component increases to $23.90 and the interest component falls to $527.30, a change of 25 cents. The outstanding balance after the payment is made is $49,952.45. Not much of a change, really. In fact, the halfway point in paying off the mortgage is not even reached until payment 238 is made — almost 20 years down the road.

Kevin and Sheri have saved up $500, a nice, round sum, and used the money to prepay the mortgage. But it is difficult for Kevin and Sheri to see precisely what they have gained by playing POPS. How does the prepayment fit into their amortization schedule? It doesn't, and the result is that a new amortization schedule would have to be ordered, reflecting the $500 prepayment. There is a better way to prepay: By prepaying in accordance with the amortization schedule instead of making a lump-sum prepayment to the lender, the amount that borrowers will save by applying the POPS principle will jump right off the page!

Prepaying in Accordance with the Amortization Schedule

Calculating the benefits from playing the POPS game is much easier than everyone thinks. In fact, armed with a ruler, a pencil, a pad of paper, the amortization schedule and a calculator (optional but preferred), people can play POPS in their own living room and see the dramatic savings right before their eyes.

To illustrate how POPS works, assume that Kevin and Sheri prepaid the principal for payment two ($23.90) on February 1, 1985 when they made their first payment. By doing so, the amount shown as the blended payment two will never have to be made, reducing the amortization by one month. Payment three on the schedule will be the new payment two, due on March 1, 1985. More importantly the interest component of payment two will never have to be paid — a savings of $527.30 just by prepaying $23.90. If no other prepayments were ever made, that small prepayment would still have saved the borrowers over 20 times its cost. By prepaying in accordance with the amortization schedule, the borrowers not only save enormous sums of money, but also vividly and dramatically see what savings arise from the prepayment.

For a prepayment in accordance with the amortization schedule to work, the funds must be paid on the exact same date as the regular monthly payment. It assumes the regular monthly payment has *already* been made before the prepayment is paid. In addition, the

amount prepaid must correspond to the exact amount of
the *principal payment only* for the desired number of
payments still to come. Totally ignore the interest component and the amount of the monthly payment. We
are only interested in upcoming principal
payments — nothing more.

How would prepayment in accordance with the
amortization schedule work on a larger scale — i.e., a
sizeable prepayment being made on a payment date during the term of the mortgage?

On a popular TV game show, "The Price Is Right,"
the person who selects the closest figure to an established price of an article, without going over, is the winner.
So, too, with the POPS game. Instead of prepaying an
exact amount (i.e., $500), the better way to prepay is to
add up the appropriate number of principal payments
that come closest to $500 without exceeding it. This is
the proper amount to prepay in accordance with the
amortization schedule.

Danny and Andrea have a $50,000 mortgage at 13%
amortized over 25 years, and have a 10% prepayment
privilege. The payments of $551.20 have been made for
almost two years. The balance after payment 24 will be
$49,357.99. On the second anniversary of the interest
adjustment date, namely January 1, 1987, they want to
prepay approximately $500. Since payment 24 will
already have been made, Danny and Andrea should
start adding up the principal components *only* (not the
blended payment) starting with the 25th payment. Running down the principal column, the total of payments
25 through 39 is $491.59, the closest figure to $500
without going over. Do not include payment 40,
because the amount being prepaid then would be
$527.20 — more than Danny and Andrea want to pay.

A prepayment of $491.59 at the end of the second year will keep the amortization schedule alive.

A slightly easier method is to run down the "Balance of Loan" column and look for the new balance ($48,857.99) that would reflect a prepayment of exactly $500. This appears between payments 39 and 40. Then move up the column to the higher figure ($48,866.40). Subtract this figure from the balance after payment 24 is made ($49,357.99) and *voila* — the proper amount to prepay to keep the amortization schedule alive has been determined — $491.59.

In addition to avoid having to order a new amortization schedule every time a prepayment is made, the beauty of prepaying in accordance with the amortization schedule is what it reveals. Automatically it can be determined that the prepayment will reduce the amortization period by 15 months — payments 25 to 39 have been eliminated. The remaining amortization is now 21 years, 9 months instead of 23 years. The savings in interest cost can automatically be determined as well, in one of two ways. The harder method is to add up the interest components of payments 25 to 39, and arrive at a total of $7,776.41. The easier method is to multiply the regular payment ($551.20) by the 15 payments eliminated, and subtract the principal prepaid from that total. In other words, $551.20 times 15 equals $8,268; subtracting $491.59 means a saving of $7,776.41 in interest. By prepaying $491.59, Danny and Andrea have eliminated 15 mortgage payments over the amortized life of the mortgage, they have saved $7,776.41 in interest costs, and they can determine, verify and audit the savings with their amortization schedule!

Before walking away in disbelief, remember again that interest is a form of rent charged for the use of money. If less is outstanding, less rent has to be paid. If $491.59 is paid at the end of the second year before it is due to be returned to the lender, no "rent" will ever have to be paid on that amount of money again. These calculations show borrowers graphically and dramatically how substantial the savings are arising from playing POPS.

All that needs to be done with the amortization schedule to keep it valid is to relabel the payment date column. Obviously payment 40 on this schedule will be the real 25th payment — so change May 1, 1988, to February 1, 1987, and continue this as far down the schedule as is desired. In all other respects the schedule is still valid, fresh and alive. It accurately reflects the division of future blended payments between principal and interest.

Some lenders insist that prepayments be made in accordance with the amortization schedule of the loan, for this very reason. Borrowers who are not obligated to adopt this approach should do so in any event, as it makes prepaying a mortgage more meaningful. Remember that prepayments made in the midst of a mortgage term do not alter the payment, but they do reduce the amortization period. Prepaying in accordance with the amortization schedule must be done on the regular monthly payment date to be effective.

Remember that the payment column is totally ignored when prepaying in accordance with the amortization schedule. Any prepayment based on the payment column means that a new amortization schedule must be obtained for the loan. A double payment made one month requires a new amortization schedule; a prepayment based on the principal component only does not.

In my practice, I recommend that borrowers send a

copy of the amortization schedule to the lender with the prepayment, explaining in a letter what they have done and how the amount being prepaid was calculated. This reduces possible confusion arising between borrower and lender in the future.

Some lawyers and notaries obtain amortization schedules for their clients, while others do not. Our office orders an amortization schedule for every mortgage processed to help borrowers understand how mortgage financing works and to encourage prepayments. While some institutional lenders issued amortization schedules years ago, that is not the case today. Considering how confusing mortgage financing is, wouldn't it make sense for banks and trust companies to issue them to their borrowers, to demystify mortgages?

17

Round Up, Young Man, Round Up!

It irks me that our financial institutions are slaves to the figures in the amortization book. Once the interest rate is set, the principal determined and the amortization selected, lenders look at the book, note the corresponding payment and use that as the amount of the monthly mortgage payment. Generally, the figure selected is nonnegotiable.

This is far from enough! To me, provided the income qualifications are met, there is no good reason why the monthly payment cannot and should not be rounded up. The amount stated in the amortization book for a certain mortgage should not be viewed as the last step in determining what a borrower should pay. Instead, the figures in the amortization book that lenders use to determine the blended payment should only be a guideline — a first step in determining what the monthly payment should be. Yet mortgage lenders constantly treat the numbers in the amortization book as if they were etched on the tablets that Moses carried with him from Mount Sinai! "Unalterable. It's company policy. Our computer can't handle what you want!" My suggestions would benefit both borrowers and lenders, and are simple as well. Perhaps that is the problem.

Once the necessary qualifications have been satisfied and the *tentative* minimum monthly payment is known, based on the information in the amortization book, borrowers should "round up" their monthly payment to the nearest $5 or $10. Never round down, even one cent, because this will cost the borrower more money in the long run. All additional money paid this way goes directly to principal, resulting in further interest savings to the borrower.

Rounding up the $551.20 payment for the 13% mortgage amortized over 25 years to $555.00 a month will save the borrower $6,376.82 over the amortized life of that mortgage — just from "rounding up." The borrower would find a round figure easier to work into a monthly budget. A "rounded up" payment also means less likelihood of an error in processing the payment, or in writing a cheque. A slightly increased cash flow would benefit the lenders, so everybody wins.

18

Throw Away The Book

Rounding up the mortgage payment should not be the final step in setting the amount to be paid by a borrower either. Provided the income qualifications continue to be satisfied, why can't the monthly payment of principal and interest be tailored to the borrower's ability to pay, irrespective of what the resulting amortization might be? It makes more sense for the payment to be consciously selected, with the amortization just "falling into place," than vice versa, which is the way that lenders presently handle the matter.

The best approach to take, once the minimum monthly payment is known, would be to throw away the amortization book completely. Instead, borrowers should choose the payment that best suits them — the payment they can best afford to make — provided it exceeds the minimum payment.

For example, Jack and Elaine need a $40,000 mortgage, and have been offered a loan at 13%. This means their payment, amortized over 25 years, would be $440.96. The taxes on the property would cost $80 a month. Using the "times 40" rule, Jack and Elaine would need to earn at least $20,838.40 to qualify for the loan ($440.96 plus $80.00) x 40.

Jack and Elaine earn $27,500. Working backwards,

the largest amount they could pay, using the "times 40" rule (see chapter 6) would be:

$$\frac{\$27,500}{40} = \$687.50, \text{ less } \$80 \text{ (taxes)} = \$607.50/\text{month}$$

According to their personal budget, Jack and Elaine could afford to pay $525.00 per month towards the mortgage. Although their loans officer offered them a mortgage with a 15-year amortization, the monthly payment being $497.21, they can still afford and want to pay more towards the mortgage each month. In the usual situation, the choice of an amortization period determines the amount of the payment. Why can't the reverse hold true, so that borrowers choose the most appropriate monthly payment, which in turn determines the amortization period for the loan? This would personalize the loan, and tailor the payment to the borrower's financial ability to pay. If Jack and Elaine were able to obtain a mortgage with a payment of $525 monthly, the amortization would be 12.93 years. Further savings and a faster payoff would result from selecting the mortgage payment in this fashion. Unfortunately, typical lender replies are "we don't offer loans with funny amortization periods." Such answers really make no sense. Even with a financial calculator, one can determine the amortization for this loan — surely programmers of mainframe computers can do so too!

Private lenders frequently will permit this kind of "rounding up," allowing borrowers to select the appropriate payment rather than having the selected amortization determine the amount of the payment. As long as they are provided with an amortization schedule that shows the breakdown of payments between interest and principal, a rounded payment will suit these lenders just fine. Only force of habit and innate conservatism prevent financial institutions from doing the same.

If the lender will not allow the desired payment to dictate the length of the amortization period, choose an amortization as close to the one that the desired payment would have produced. In Jack and Elaine's case, an amortization of 13 years (if available) would produce a payment of $523.95 — an acceptable solution, but still not the best answer.

Don't be a slave! Select the amount you want to pay!

19

Increase That Mortgage Payment!

For many years, lenders would not permit any increase in the amount of the monthly payment over the term of the mortgage. Conventional mortgages were fixed rate, fixed payment, 25-year amortized contracts. This meant the hardest payment for borrowers to make was the first payment. Despite future increases in salary, all mortgage payments over the term of the loan would be the same as when the mortgage was originally arranged. In later years, a smaller percentage of gross income would be applied towards the payment of the mortgage for this reason.

Keeping mortgage payments fixed made little sense from a borrower's point of view. Salary increases recognized that *all* aspects of the cost of living rose with inflation. While borrowers received extra money to pay for the higher costs being encountered in the marketplace, effectively they were shut out from applying any of these funds to the cost of financing their shelter.

Recently, some lenders have begun accepting a voluntary regular "step-up" in monthly mortgage payments at little or no cost, depending on the lender. Generally, one increase is allowed per year, at any time during the year. Find out from the lender, *before the mortgage is booked*, whether, when and how the monthly payment can be increased, and by what amount.

Since the entire increase in the monthly payment is applied directly to reduce the amount of principal outstanding on the mortgage, the benefits of increased payments are substantial. Looking at our standard $50,000 mortgage at 13% amortized over 25 years, the monthly payment will be $551.20. If the payment was increased permanently by 10% at the end of the first year, and nothing else was done, the new payment of $606.32 would reduce the total amortization to 16.89 years, and the total interest costs drop from $115,367.71 to $74,514.15. If the payment was increased by only 5% each and every year, the loan would be paid off in under 12 years, and the total interest cost would be reduced to $54,054.40 These savings result from just a nominal increase in the monthly payment.

Before restructuring the amount of the monthly mortgage payment, see if the lender levies an administrative charge for doing this. While the charge may be nominal in comparison to the savings earned, it may deter some borrowers, expecially those planning to make a small increase in their payment.

Hope is not lost for those borrowers who are not permitted to increase their fixed regular monthly mortgage payments. Instead of increasing their mortgage payments directly with their lender, the same result can be achieved *indirectly* by borrowing money from another source, and prepaying the borrowed money to the lender as allowed by the prepayment privilege in most mortgages. As wild an idea as it sounds — borrowing to prepay — the benefits are both clear and sizeable. See chapter 21.

20

Shorter Amortizations Are Better — Here's Proof!

The amortization for a mortgage is the period of time over which the entire principal will be retired if no prepayment and no late payments are made. Conventional mortgages had amortizations of 25 years, blindly accepted for generations by Canadian borrowers. Since all mortgages are front-end loaded, today's high interest rates mean that even less principal is paid off in the early years of the loan. For example, at the end of the first year the following amounts are paid off on a $50,000 mortgage amortized over 25 years at various interest rates:

10%	*11%*	*12%*	*13%*	*14%*	*15%*
$489.57	$417.26	$354.76	$300.82	$254.62	$214.98

Higher interest rates not only cost more, but accomplish less as the loan is paid increasingly slowly in its early years.

How much is accomplished by reducing the amortization for a mortgage? Much depends on the interest rate charged for the loan. On the chart below, I have made the assumption that at least 1% of the outstanding principal should be repaid the first year of the loan. On a $50,000 loan, for example, at least $500 should be repaid during the first year of the loan. The heavy black line (called the Silverstein line) shows the amortization that accomplishes this for given interest rates. All amortizations to the left of the line surpass this test; all amortizations to the right of the line do not accomplish this.

For example, at 10%, an amortization between 24 and 25 years will result in $500 being repaid to the lender the first year. At 12%, the amortization is between 22 and 23 years. For 15% mortgages, the figure rests between 19 and 20 years. Amortizations shorter than these will surpass the desired result; longer amortizations will not.

What does all this mean? Simply put, it provides borrowers with a sound, rational basis for selecting a maximum amortization period. Because mortgage payments are heavily interest laden, borrowers want to see the results of their payments. They want to know that the money paid each month has made a noticeable dent in reducing their outstanding indebtedness. While a 1% reduction in the outstanding principal the first year of the loan is an arbitrary figure, it is not an unrealistic goal to strive for. Nor does it put an onerous burden on borrowers. Instead, the Silverstein line clearly shows borrowers and lenders the maximum amortization period to select in order to see a significant growth in equity resulting from the mortgage payments made.

Whenever possible, stay to the left of the Silverstein line. Borrowers who do will be glad they did.

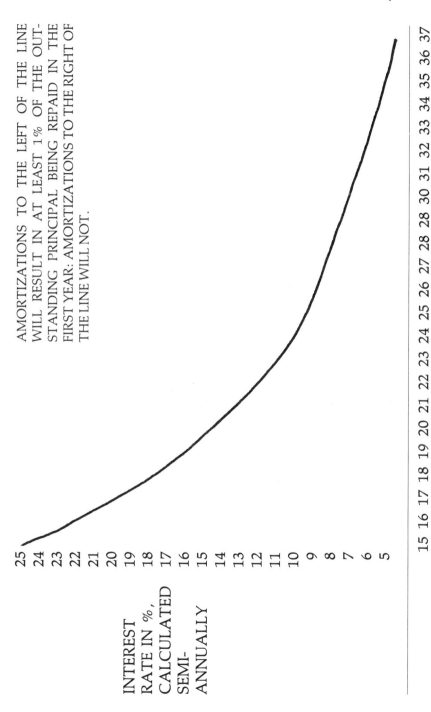

AMORTIZATIONS TO THE LEFT OF THE LINE WILL RESULT IN AT LEAST 1% OF THE OUT-STANDING PRINCIPAL BEING REPAID IN THE FIRST YEAR: AMORTIZATIONS TO THE RIGHT OF THE LINE WILL NOT.

INTEREST RATE IN %, CALCULATED SEMI-ANNUALLY

AMORTIZATION IN YEARS

21

Borrowing To Prepay

Many mortgages, especially those issued by financial institutions, permit some limited right of prepayment. Although borrowers would like to take advantage of POPS, they may find themselves lacking sufficient funds to make a lump-sum prepayment when the mortgage "opens up." Others would like to increase their monthly payment to reflect an increase in salary over the previous year. Unfortunately, their lender will not permit this. A solution exists to both situations — borrowing to prepay. As ludicrous as it appears, using Peter's money to prepay Paul can save enormous sums of money.

Glen and Donna can prepay up to 10% of their mortgage on April 1 each year. Their three-year mortgage was booked at $50,000 at 13% amortized over 25 years, with payments of $551.20 monthly. No increase in payments is allowed. During the year, their salaries increased by 8%, so they could pay another $45 or so each month and still be paying roughly the same percentage of their income towards their mortgage. They would like to play the POPS game, but do not have too much ready cash in the bank. Sound familiar?

At the end of the first year of their mortgage, Glen and Donna would owe $49,699.18. Consider what would happen if they borrowed just $500, and paid 16% per annum calculated monthly for that loan, to be repaid and amortized over one year. Note that the interest rate on this loan is 3% higher than their mortgage rate, and is calculated monthly, not semi-annually. The new loan would cost them an additional $45.37 each month, for a total of $596.57 — quite close to the 8% increase in salary they are receiving. By prepaying the $500 borrowed at the end of the first year, Glen and Donna will save $8,930.22 in interest costs. The interest cost on the $500 loan over the one-year term is only $44.38. In other words, by borrowing $500 at a higher rate and prepaying it at the end of the first year, the $44.38 investment that Glen and Donna made would save them over 200 times that amount.

If they wanted to prepay in acccordance with the amortization schedule, they would have to add a further $28.59 of their own money to the $500 being borrowed. From the amortization schedule they would learn that the combined prepayment would save them $9,393.01.

Lucy and Ricky have written employment contracts that guarantee them a 5% salary increase next year. They would like to prepay $1,000 towards their mortgage on July 1, the anniversary date of their mortgage and the only date that prepayments are allowed. Their salary increases will not take effect until January 1 of next year. Two years have already passed on their $50,000 mortgage at 13% amortized over 25 years, and they have never prepaid the mortgage to date. The cost of borrowing the $1,000 at 16.5% calculated monthly for 1 year will be $91.67. By prepaying the $1,000 towards the mortgage now, they reduce the remaining interest cost on the mortgage from $101,780.92 to $87,143.65, a savings of $14,637.27. Quite a good rate of return on Lucy and Ricky's investment. Considering their marginal tax bracket (35%), they would have to earn $22,518.87 in income to pay off this amount. All for a cost of less than $100 in interest costs for the year!

Borrowing to play the POPS game reflects the fact that mortgages are front-end loaded, the heaviest interest costs being in the early years of the loan. If the term and the amortization of the new loan are only for one year, so that the loan is repaid by the next prepayment date when the scheme can be used again, some of the money owing on the long-term amortized mortgage is being repaid by a loan with a shorter amortization. In the early years of a mortgage, borrowing to prepay will reduce substantially the overall interest cost of the mortgage, even if the money to prepay the loan is borrowed at a rate of interest higher than the mortgage interest rate.

Borrowing to prepay may be the only method open to borrowers who would like to increase their monthly mortgage payments to match an increase in salary, but who cannot do so directly under the terms of their mortgage. What could not be accomplished directly is being accomplished indirectly.

Don't let a prepayment opportunity go by without using it. Sit down and calculate if a little larger amount can be paid next year on a monthly basis than was paid last year. If so, then consider borrowing to prepay the loan, and increase the monthly payment indirectly to finance the prepayment. The benefits are staggering.

22

A Dollar A Day Is A-OK!

An old expression familiar to everyone is "an apple a day keeps the doctor away!" Ever wonder what setting aside just a dollar a day and prepaying it towards the mortgage will do?

Mike and Gloria put a dollar a day into a non-interest bearing shoe-box starting right after their mortgage was arranged. The $365 was prepaid to the lender as a prepayment on each anniversary date. The original loan was $50,000 at 13% amortized over 25 years. Nothing else was ever done to reduce the amortization. Surprise! The loan was retired in full in just over 19 years, and the interest savings to them was $39,026.89. Not bad for loose change or "munch" money!

Archie and Edith were a little wiser, and *each* put a dollar into an old sock. The savings — $64,603.20 and a mortgage paid off in a little over 15 years!

The odds of winning sure beat those of a lottery! And the winnings are guaranteed!

23

A Little Less Borrowed, A Lot More Saved

Home owners who are refinancing and buyers who are arranging mortgages can benefit from an interesting "trick" that highlights one of the key differences between Canadian and American mortgages. In Canada, a sum of money is borrowed and the first mortgage payment is made one month or more after closing, "not in advance." Instead, borrowers should pretend they reside in the United States. There, mortgage payments are made "in advance," meaning the first mortgage payment is due and payable when the mortgage proceeds are received. The net advance already has the first mortgage payment deducted. To apply this approach, Canadian borrowers should borrow the amount of money otherwise needed *less* the amount of the first payment. Everything else stays the same. The results are startling.

Kenny and Elaine did this. They were going to borrow $50,000 at 13% amortized over 25 years with payments of $551.20. By imagining that they were in the USA, they borrowed only $49,448.80. This was the amount they originally intended to borrow less one payment of $551.20. Of course, this is the net advance an American borrower would have received on closing. The result: an amortization reduced to 23.25 years, just like that, with an interest savings of $11,548.13. The true north strong and mortgage-free — sooner!

24

Playing Leap Frog With A Mortgage

Everyone played leap frog as a kid. As we grow older, it just does not seem appropriate to play a kids' game like that. Not so when a mortgage is outstanding! Playing leap frog with a mortgage according to the amortization schedule is a nice, easy way to save large sums of money. Everyone with any prepayment privilege in his mortgage can play leap frog, and constantly win.

The basic idea behind leap frog is to pay the odd numbered regular mortgage payments and to prepay the even numbered payments. That's all! Obviously, since two payments are made at once, the loan will be paid off in half the time — 12½ years for a 25-year amortized loan. How does playing leap frog with a mortgage really work?

Howard and Sheila have a $50,000 mortgage identical to the one Kevin and Sheri have. See Appendix B for the Amortization Schedule. On February 1, 1985, they paid the regular mortgage payment of $551.20 (payment 1) and prepaid the principal portion of payment 2 ($23.90). On March 1, 1985, they paid the regular mortgage payment of $551.20 (payment 3 on the schedule) and prepaid the principal portion of payment 4 ($24.40). And so on. The payment due on January 1,

1986 is payment 23 ($551.20) while the principal portion of payment 24 is prepaid ($30.10). After one year of payments, Howard and Sheila have retired 24 payments from the schedule.

Where do the prepayments go? If the mortgage is fully open, the prepayment (the even numbered principal payments) *must* be sent to the lender each month, together with the regular monthly payment. It must be received on time each month, and must properly clear the bank. Not all mortgages are fully open, though, and in fact, very few are. What are borrowers who have closed mortgages to do?

No need to fret! What they should do is open up a daily-interest savings account. On the day the mortgage payment is due, the "leap frogged amount" (the principal portion of the evenly numbered payments) is paid into the account. In other words, on February 1, 1985, Howard and Sheila would pay $23.90 into the daily-interest savings account. On March 1, 1985, $24.40 would be paid into the account. And so on.

The lender has been receiving his normal mortgage payments every month. The "leap frogging" has been taking place in another account. How does the lender get the amount that has been "leap frogged"? On the first anniversary date of the mortgage, namely January 1, 1986, when a prepayment is permitted, money has to be paid to the lender to bring everything up to date. Since the lender has only received twelve mortgage payments and no prepayments, according to his records only $300.82 in principal has been paid to date. This is one full year's worth of principal payments. From the borrower's point of view, two full years' worth of payments have left his hands — one year's payments to the lender, and one year's principal payments to the "leap frog account." To coordinate everything, $341.19 must be paid to the lender on January 1, 1986. This is the amount of the principal payments for the mortgage in its second full year. It is identical to the amount that the borrower with a fully open loan would have paid to the borrower in the year. Then the slate is clean. Then one year's worth of regular monthly payments, together with one year's worth of "leap-frogged" prepayments will have been paid to the lender. By doing this, two years' worth of payments will have been eliminated from the amortization schedule in just twelve months.

If the daily-interest savings account paid interest monthly at 8% per annum calculated annually, the amount in the daily-interest account as of January 1, 1986 would be $334.04, made up of $322.69 paid into the account and $11.35 accrued interest. But $341.19 has to be paid on January 1, 1986 for the leap-frogged prepayment to be correct. To bring everything up-to-date in accordance with the amortization schedule, Howard and Sheila would have to take $7.15 from their own pocket, and add it to the amount in the leap-frog account when prepaying the mortgage.

What does all this mean? First, borrowers with fully open mortgages need not open a special bank account to play leap frog. Secondly, all other borrowers can play leap frog, but will have to take a nominal sum of money out of their own pocket to bring everything "up-to-date" each year. This can be considered the charge for not having a fully open mortgage. Most importantly, by playing leap frog according to the amortization schedule in this fashion, borrowers can retire their mortgage debt in half the time.

Playing leap frog with a mortgage sounds crazy, but it's so satisfying!

25

Weekly Mortgages

At first glance, the thought of paying mortgages weekly or every two weeks (for simplicity called weekly mortgages) sounds overwhelming, or perhaps too unconventional. Mortgages traditionally have been payable monthly, and little attention has ever been given to changing this. Yet there is no magic in monthly mortgage payments. Since few people are paid monthly, it would make more sense to tailor the frequency of mortgage payments to a borrower's pay period. Weekly and bi-weekly mortgages (also known as fast-pay mortgages) do just that. The added benefit to borrowers is how dramatically fast-pay mortgages reduce the long-term interest costs of home mortgages. Weekly mortgages are an excellent example of POPS.

When is a fast-pay mortgage appropriate? The answer is in its application. For a simple example, if the blended monthly payment of principal and interest is $400, is the borrower prepared to pay $100 weekly or $200 every two weeks? If so, then the borrower should consider the fast-pay scheme. Note that the same interest rate applies to both weekly and monthly mortgage payments.

Two different approaches exist with regard to calculating weekly mortgages — one which greatly benefits borrowers, the other which does little to reduce the interest costs of a loan. One involves paying the same *monthly* amount on a weekly, bi-weekly or semi-monthly basis, while the other is based on paying the same *annual* amount on a weekly or bi-weekly basis.

The chart opposite highlights the savings that result from fast-pay mortgages. The interest rate is 13%, calculated semi-annually, not in advance.

The first column is the yardstick by which fast-pay mortgages must be compared, namely the conventional mortgage. Columns II, III and IV show the effects of fast-pay mortgages payable weekly, bi-weekly (every two weeks) and semi-monthly (twice a month), when the *annual* total of principal and interest is paid more frequently than monthly. The savings to borrowers in terms of a lower amortization as well as a reduction in interest costs are nominal indeed. Remember that at all times the interest rate, despite the scheme, is still 13%, calculated semi-annually, not in advance.

Columns V and VI show the impact of fast-pay mortgages where the amount of the *monthly* payment is paid more frequently. One-quarter of it is paid weekly in column V and one-half of it is paid every two weeks in column VI. Looking at column V, if a weekly payment of $137.80 was made by the borrower, everything else remaining the same, the total interest cost would be reduced to $70,586.60 — a savings of $44,781.11 or almost 39% of the total interest cost. The loan will be paid off in under 17 years as well. All of this is achieved by paying one-quarter of the normal monthly payment each week, without any change in the interest rate charged by the lender or the manner in which interest is calculated.

Similar savings result from bi-weekly payments of $275.60 (column VI). The total interest cost would be

	I Conventional mortgage monthly payment	II Annual amount paid in 52 weekly instalments	III Annual amount paid in 26 bi-weekly instalments	IV Annual amount paid in 24 semi-monthly instalments	V Monthly amount paid in 4 weekly instalments	VI Monthly amount paid in 2 bi-weekly instalments
Payments	$551.20	$127.20	$254.40	$275.60	$137.80	$275.60
Amortized life of the loan	25 years	24.32 years	24.52 years	24.55 years	16.83 years	16.90 years
Interest cost	$115,367.71	$110,843.25	$112,157.68	$112,380.21	$70,586.60	$71,094.32
Interest saved over conventional loan	NIL	$4,521.46	$3,210.03	$2,987.50	$44,781.11	$44,273.39
Extra principal paid annually	NIL	NIL	NIL	NIL	$551.20	$551.20

NOTE: The monthly amount paid in two semi-monthly instalments is exactly the same as column IV.

$71,094.32, saving the borrower $44,273.39. The loan is retired in just under 17 years. Again, this has been achieved merely by altering the frequency of payments and nothing more.

Clearly, borrowers benefit greatly when the *monthly* payment is used in establishing the amount of the fast-pay mortgage payment.

How does a simple shift in payment lead to such enormous savings for borrowers? The answer is two-fold. With more payments being made annually (52 as opposed to 12), the outstanding principal is being reduced faster than normal, resulting in an accelerated reduction of principal. It is similar to a bank account — depositing one dollar per week into a daily interest savings account is worth more than merely depositing four dollars at the end of the same four-week period. The greater the frequency of payments, the greater the compounding effect.

More important, however, is the built-in prepayment that weekly mortgages provide. While there are 12 months in a year, there are 13 four-week periods in that same year. With a blended payment of $400 per month, the borrower would be paying $4,800 annually. With a blended payment of $100 a week, the borrower will be paying $5,200 during that same year. By paying one-quarter of a conventional monthly payment each week to the lender, the borrower in effect is prepaying one extra mortgage payment to the lender each year. Columns V and VI clearly show that the equivalent of one extra mortgage payment is made annually. Prepayments, even when made this way, go directly to reduce the outstanding principal. They also will reduce the amortization for the loan, if the amount borrowed and the interest rate are kept constant. When the built-in annual prepayment is added to the effect of the additional number of payments made annually, the results are truly astounding.

The beauty of the scheme is in its simplicity. It is not a complicated plan like variable rate mortgages. All that borrowers have to do is divide the conventional payment by four (or two for payments made every two weeks). No additional costs need to be incurred. It is very simple to calculate the weekly mortgage payment, and of great benefit to the vast majority of people who would rather forego the finer points of mortgage financing. Weekly mortgages will prove useful for family budgets since mortgage payments are coordinated with paydays. Plainly and simply, weekly mortgages are viewed by the public as an alternative method of making mortgage payments, but one that substantially reduces the interest cost of a loan at no extra charge.

Amortization schedules are now available that show the proper breakdown of principal and interest each week, including the proper day for each payment. This is an invaluable aid to both lenders and borrowers, and is one of the reasons why weekly mortgages are gaining increased acceptance.

A number of financial institutions have now adopted the fast-pay scheme in Canada. Some have opted only for bi-weekly mortgages as the extra administrative costs, in their view, do not justify the nominal savings of weekly payments compared to bi-weekly payments. Careful shopping is needed, as with any area of mortgage financing.

Do not be swayed by some of the "alternatives" proposed by lending institutions either. A popular alternative is to accumulate the extra income in a daily interest savings account and to make a lump-sum prepayment each year. None of these plans work as effectively to the home owner's advantage as do weekly mortgages. Also, make sure that the amount to be paid weekly or every two weeks is based on the *monthly* payment and not the amount paid annually. Otherwise, little will be achieved from the increased frequency of payments.

Work that I have done on this topic in the United States indicates that Americans are keenly interested in reducing their interest costs through weekly mortgages as well, even though interest costs there are deductable from income. With Canada's tax laws not permitting the interest cost of home mortgages to be deducted except in limited circumstances, an additional compelling reason exists to adopt this scheme. Weekly mortgage payments have now been perceived by the Canadian public as an innovative answer to the problems of high interest rates, large mortgage payments and huge interest costs. The ever-increasing number of financial institutions offering this scheme is proof positive that the Canadian public is being heard, loud and clear. As a simple, effective means of promoting the POPS principle without altering interest rates, weekly mortgages are a viable alternative available to a large number of Canadians that should not be overlooked.

26

Combine And Conquer

Many interesting ideas and novel ways of prepaying mortgages according to the POPS principle have been presented in this book. With a little advance planning, the application of these concepts will help both home owners and home buyers substantially save on high interest costs and considerably shorten the amortization period. Consider the benefits to borrowers if they coupled some of these approaches!

To buy their house, Mark and Pam borrowed $50,000 on a mortgage at 13%, amortized over 25 years. Monthly payment: $551.20. This loan would cost them $115,367.71 over the amortized life of the mortgage. Pam's twin, Judy, and her husband Michael bought the identical house, but were able to skrimp and save an extra $1,000 for closing, so their mortgage was only $49,000. They also amortized their mortgage over 20 years, the monthly payment being $562.29. Net cost to them over the 20-year amortized life of the loan: $85,949.46. This meant that Michael and Judy saved $29,418.25 just by paying a further $1,000 on closing and by amortizing the loan over 20 rather than 25 years. Yet the additional monthly carrying cost to do this was only $11.09, or 36.5¢ per day!

Ward and June went much further. They went all the way! When arranging a $50,000 mortgage at 13% amortized over 25 years, they adopted weekly instead of monthly payments. In addition, they rounded up the payment from $137.40 the first year to $140. At the end of the first year, they prepaid $500, which came from putting a dollar a day into the bank as well as their income tax refunds. In all subsequent years they increased their weekly payment by a nominal amount. Larger prepayments were also made on each subsequent anniversary date, reflecting the increases in salary Ward and June received. The following is a list of what Ward and June did with their mortgage:

Year	Weekly Payment	Amount Prepaid at the End of the Year
Year 1	$140.00	$500.00
Year 2	$150.00	$530.00
Year 3	$160.00	$565.00
Year 4	$170.00	$595.00
Year 5	$185.00	$625.00
Year 6	$195.00	$660.00
Year 7	$205.00	$695.00
Year 8	$220.00	$730.00
Year 9	$230.00	Nil

By adopting:
1. Weekly payments
2. Rounded up payments
3. Increased payments in subsequent years
4. Lump-sum prepayments; and
5. Increased prepayments in subsequent years

Ward and June were able to pay off their loan, originally amortized over 25 years, in eight years and eight months. The total interest cost to them: $31,198.75, as opposed to the original amortization cost of $115,367.92, a savings of $84,169.17! As they are in the 33 1/3% tax bracket, the savings to them in before-tax dollars is $126,253.76. Now the money they had been spending on mortgage payments could be spent for other purposes — trips, clothes, a new car, and so on.

Thousands of borrowers are reducing their after-tax dollar interest costs and shortening their amortizations by adopting one or more of these ideas. Don't wait any longer! Join in!

27

Your Statutory Right To Prepay

The misconception that all mortgages can be prepaid with three months' penalty appears to have arisen with *s. 10* of the *Interest Act of Canada*, and comparable provincial legislation such as *s. 17* of the *Mortgages Act of Ontario*. These sections impose a three-hurdle test that must be met before a statutory right of prepayment is permitted.

1. *Who took out the mortgage — an individual or a corporation?*

If an individual was the original borrower, the first hurdle has been met. If the original borrower was a corporation, it's game over, even if the mortgage has been assumed by an individual. With newly constructed homes, the corporate builder often arranges the mortgage and is the original borrower. The home owner assumes or takes over the mortgage on closing. In this situation, no statutory right to prepay exists.

Elliott and Michelle, and Irv and Lillian, purchased a home from Better Homes Limited. Elliott and Michelle arranged their mortgage directly with the Bank of Thornhill. If the second and third questions can be properly answered, then their statutory right to prepay exists. In Irv and Lillian's situation, the mortgage with the Bank of Thornhill was arranged by Better Homes

Limited, which signed the original mortgage with the Bank. Irv and Lillian on closing assumed that mortgage, and agreed to be bound by all of its terms. Nevertheless, even if the other two hurdles can be met, Irv and Lillian have no statutory right to prepay.

Check the original mortgage to verify who the original borrower was. If in doubt, get a copy of the original mortgage from the land registry office. The name of the original borrower should appear near the top of first page of the mortgage.

2. *Is the period of time from the signing of the original mortgage to its maturity more than five years?*
This is the crucial question. When the mortgage was signed is the key date, as the clock starts to run from that point in time. When interest adjustment dates are used (see chapter 9), the mortgage could have been signed anywhere from one to 30 days before the interest adjustment date. This is how borrowers are able to squeeze under the wire. If the original mortgage term was five years "plus" (including the time from the signing of the mortgage to the interest adjustment date), head for hurdle three. If the time from signing to maturity is less than five years or is exactly five years to the day, forget it. No statutory right to prepay exists.

Renewals must be ignored. They cannot be added to the original term to satisfy the statutory requirement. The original term itself is the key. It must be for more than five years to qualify for the statutory right to prepay. The mortgage arranged by Fred and Ethel ran from September 1, 1980 to September 1, 1985. They cannot rely on the statutory prepayment privilege, no matter how long the renewal period, as their original term did not exceed five years; it was exactly five years.

Cole and Melissa arranged a mortgage starting August 29, 1980, having an interest adjustment date of September 1, 1980, maturity being September 1, 1984. Because the original mortgage term was four years and three days, the mortgage does not qualify for the statutory prepayment right, even if the mortgage was coupled to a two-year renewal at 17% to September 1, 1986. If they wish to prepay this loan, they are left to the whim and discretion of the lender. Darryl and Kylie also arranged a mortgage starting August 29, 1980 with an interest adjustment date of September 1, 1980. Their mortgage matured on September 1, 1985. As the original term was five years and three days, Darryl and Kylie do have a statutory right to prepay during their one-year renewal term at 17% to September 1, 1986. Even though the renewals mature on the same day, only the mortgage with an *original* term of five years "plus" can invoke this statutory right. Harsh but true.

3. *Have at least five years passed since the mortgage was signed?*
Even though the first two hurdles may have been met, at least five years must have passed before the section becomes operative. Typically, the mortgage for the "five years plus" has been renewed, and the desire to invoke the statutory prepayment right arises during the renewal term.

Aaron and Frieda arranged their own mortgage, running from June 20, 1983, having an interest adjustment date of July 1, 1983 and a maturity date of July 1, 1988. Only after July 1, 1988 can they rely on the statutory right to prepay. As the mortgage is fully open in any event on July 1, 1988, they could only rely on this right during a renewal of the mortgage.

Rick and Sharon's mortgage of five years and three days matured on July 1, 1984. Regardless of how long a period their mortgage was renewed for, they can rely on the statutory right to prepay their mortgage during the renewal term, since more than five years have passed since the mortgage was signed.

It should be noted that if a mortgage qualifies for the statutory right of prepayment, it can be repaid in whole (but not in part) upon payment of a penalty totalling three months' interest.

Many Canadians looked at the statutory right to prepay as their salvation after renewing their mortgages during the period of high interest rates in the early 1980s. Unfortunately, the availability of this statutory right has been somewhat exaggerated. As the original term (excluding renewals) must exceed five years, not all *existing* mortgages qualified. As Fred and Ethel and Cole and Melissa learned, the statutory right of prepayment does not apply to mortgages renewed with the same lender at extremely high interest rates if the original mortgage term was five years or less. With the trend to shorter-term mortgages, fewer *new* five-year mortgages are being booked as well. Lenders have also added a new wrinkle, by shortening their five year mortgage terms to 59 months! That's right — five years have only 59 months. Clayton and Ellie learned this when they arranged their mortgage. Although their five-year mortgage started to run on June 20, 1983, having an interest adjustment date of July 1, 1983, the maturity was June 1, 1988 — 59 months later. In this way, the lender ensured that the total term, including the period prior to the interest adjustment date, is less than five years. If this had not been done, Clayton and Ellie's mortgage would have qualified for the statutory right to prepay, by having an original term of five years and ten days.

What has aroused the ire of many Canadians recently is the requirement of some institutional lenders that borrowers on their renewal waive any statutory prepayment privileges they otherwise might have had. Only those prepayment privileges stated in the renewal document would be permitted. Typically, these changes were not brought to the attention of the borrowers when they signed the renewal. Instead, they were buried in the body of the renewal document. The question as to whether borrowers can waive their statutory prepayment privileges in this manner presently is being challenged in the Courts.

Things are a lot different today than yesterday. Renewals aren't just renewals any more — they may contain new rules governing the relationship between the parties, forcing borrowers to give up some of the rights afforded to them by law. If in doubt as to whether any statutory prepayment rights exist which are being waived, take the renewal document to a lawyer immediately before signing it! Don't assume anything!

28

Variable (Adjustable) Rate Mortgages

As a child, I remember being told of the evils of gambling. In today's mortgage market, choosing the right mortgage term and the right mortgage rate is a big enough gamble. Once the decision is made, borrowers must live with it — good or bad. Variable rate mortgages (VRMs) are for the real shooters — those who like to live dangerously, who like to gamble frequently, who believe interest rates will fall and who are prepared to put their money where their mouth is. And yet, despite all the negatives that have been expressed about VRMs, they are a practical alternative in certain circumstances.

With a fixed rate mortgage, the rate is etched in stone for the term of the mortgage. Not so with a VRM. While the term of the mortgage may be anywhere from one to five years, the rate floats and can change ("be adjusted") as frequently as every month, based on the cost of money in the marketplace. What a VRM does is pass the risk of fluctuating interest rates directly to the borrower. Plainly stated, interest is paid every month at current rates to the lender. Of course, VRMs were a child of the period of high interest rates, when lenders found it impossible to properly match savings funds coming in with mortgage funds being lent out. VRMs guarantee to the lender the interest "spread" the lender needs to operate.

Like most mortgage products, the specific terms of VRMs differ from lender to lender. A number of similarities do exist, though. Most VRMs are fully open, or open with a fixed penalty. This is to be expected since the interest rate on the VRM at the time of the prepayment is the current market rate. Lenders do not suffer, for the prepaid funds can be re-lent at current rates. Longer-term mortgages are also possible. With the interest rate being adjusted frequently during the term of the mortgage, the "matching principle," discussed in Chapter 10, is always satisfied. A 25-year mortgage term could easily be granted for this reason, although few lenders' terms exceed five years. Because interest rates could change as often as every month, interest is calculated monthly and not semi-annually. As such, the rate effectively is higher than that quoted for fixed rate mortgages. (Remember: compare apples and apples, not apples and oranges; 13% calcuated monthly is equivalent to 13.357% calculated semi-annually.)

Despite this, the interest rate on a VRM is generally lower than that of conventional mortgages. In periods of inflation, fixed mortgage interest rates contain an inflation factor — a premium for inflation added to the cost of borrowing funds. When inflation is running at higher than normal levels, or it is feared this will happen, lenders can and do include an additional charge to cover the risk that inflation will continue to escalate, and that the cost of borrowing funds will be even higher in the near future. With a VRM, this latter component never has to be included in the setting of a mortgage rate, since the adjustable rate always keeps pace with both inflation and the cost of borrowing money.

How VRMs Work

With a VRM, the initial mortgage payment is set in the same fashion as a conventional mortgage, with the interest rate calculated monthly. Therefore, with a $50,000 loan amortized over 25 years, at current interest rates of 15%, the payment will be $640.42 monthly. Although the interest rate may change, the monthly payment remains fixed for the term of the mortgage. Some lenders will allow a graduated "step-up" in payments, if negotiated at the outset.

If interest rates fall during the term of the mortgage, more money will be paid each month than otherwise would be the case. This extra money goes towards reducing the outstanding principal. This extra money, in effect, is a prepayment of money and reduces both the interest cost and the amortization for the loan. On the other hand, if interest rates rise during the term of the mortgage, less money will be paid each month than is necessary to amortize the loan over 25 years. More of the monthly payment needs to be applied towards interest. In fact, and this is the problem, if interest rates rise dramatically, the monthly payment may not even be sufficient to cover the outstanding interest for the month. If this happens, then the unpaid interest is added to the outstanding principal — called negative amortization — and borrowers could end up owing more money than at the start. With this erosion in equity, the borrower could be asked to make a higher payment, to make a lump-sum payment to be applied towards the outstanding principal, or to pay off the loan in full.

Benny and Debbie plan on taking out the VRM discussed above, and want to know what would happen if interest rates were 1% higher and 1% lower for the first year of the loan. Monthly payments would be $640.42.

	Amount of Interest Paid	Amount Principal Reduced By	Principal after One Year
At 15% (no change)	$7,486.73	$198.31	$49,801.69
At 14% (rate down 1%)	$6,954.29	$730.75	$49,269.25
At 16% (rate up 1%)	$7,685.04	($339.16)	$50,339.16

At 16%, all money paid went towards interest. In addition, an additional $339.16 was added to the principal. Not a game for the weak of heart!

Several other points should be noted about VRMs. The outstanding principal could very easily increase and equity be eroded if interest rates rise, so most lenders will not loan up to 75% of the appraised value. Many will use 66% to 70% as the maximum amount of financing they will give. The Gross Debt Service and Total Debt Service ratios may be lower, meaning a higher income is needed to qualify for the loan. Most lenders will only grant VRMs as first mortgages, requiring that any possible second lender acknowledge that the principal on the first mortgage can increase, depending on where interest rates go. Finally, most lenders will allow borrowers with VRMs to lock into a conventional fixed rate mortgage at any time, upon payment of the standard "administration fee," which differs from lender to lender. Some charge a flat fee, others a sum reducing with time, while others will require a new mortgage to be prepared and registered.

When Should a VRM Be Considered?

Spawned by inflation, VRMs are worth considering as an alternative to fixed rate mortgages when interest rates are excessively high. It is hoped those days are long past! With drops in interest rates benefiting borrowers, VRMs are a practical method of "riding out the storm" of higher interest rates, whether on a purchase or on a mortgage renewal. To make VRMs worthwhile, it is important to try to book the VRM at the crest of the interest rate cycle, or on the downward curve. If rates go up after the VRM is booked, even ever so slightly, negative amortization would take hold if the payment is not large enough to cover the interest portion of the loan. While all might work out to the borrower's benefit in the long run, knowing that more money is owing than at the beginning is an ill feeling indeed. Yet, who knows if a quoted rate is the peak, or just a rest-stop on the way to the top?

Surprisingly, some borrowers are also keen on VRMs when interest rates are very low. Their argument goes this way. If the cost of locking into a conventional mortgage is nominal, better they should benefit from the lower rates that VRMs provide. If and when rates rise, that is the time to lock into a conventional mortgage. While there is some validity to this argument, it runs counter to what most people would do during a period of low interest rates!

29

Second Mortgages

The thought of taking out a second mortgage, for whatever purpose, causes ill feelings for most borrowers. Some argue that second mortgages are the first step in heading towards financial disaster, a sure sign of financial insecurity. While home buyers and home owners might feel more secure with only one mortgage, the number of mortgages outstanding against a property is not the key factor. Rather, what they should be concerned about is the dollar value of the mortgages registered against their property, and conversely, how much equity they still have in the property. A home owner's equity in his house is still $25,000, based on a fair market value of $100,000, whether one mortgage for $75,000, two mortgages for $60,000 and $15,000 respectively, two mortgages for $50,000 and $25,000, or three mortgages for $45,000, $20,000 and $10,000 be registered against the title to the property. In all of these cases, 75% of our elastic pie is held by other people, while the owner's share is the remaining 25%.

The rate to be paid for the second mortgage will depend on the owner's equity as well. If the first and second mortgages do not exceed 75% of the appraised value, the second mortgage really is almost as secure as a conventional first mortgage, and the rate charged should reflect this. When the owner's equity is less than 25%, the second mortgage will have to bear a much higher rate of interest, depending on the security, the covenant and the lender.

Second mortgages are riskier for lenders, but that is not our concern. On the other hand, second mortgages could be an effective way of reducing the high interest costs associated with residential mortgages, especially if money is needed only for a short-term purpose.

Ian and Marie owe $50,000 on a first mortgage at 13% amortized over 25 years. Their monthly payment is $551.20. The total interest cost for this loan would be $115,367.92. If they would like an additional $10,000 for home improvements, renovations (the "equity loan"), or to finance a university education, two options are open to them:

1. Arrange a new $60,000 first mortgage; or
2. Arrange a new $10,000 second mortgage.

The rates quoted for the two options are 13% for the new first mortgage, and 16% for the second mortgage. Before automatically assuming the new first mortgage route is cheaper, advance planning is needed. Will the premature payment of the old first mortgage lead to a sizeable prepayment penalty? If Ian and Marie stay with the same lender, no prepayment penalty should be incurred, since more funds are being advanced to them on the same property. This ties their hands considerably, though, because it means that they cannot look at other lender's terms and rates without incurring a sizeable prepayment penalty. Before they do anything at all, they would be wise to learn what the penalty would be for shifting their business elsewhere, and to get it in writing.

If a new $60,000 mortgage was arranged, the additional $10,000 would cost Ian and Marie $23,073.59 based on an increase in the monthly payment of $110.24, from $551.20 to $661.44.

Even though second mortgages are calculated monthly (a key difference) and their interest rates generally are at least 2% higher than first mortgages, this still could be the cheaper route for Ian and Marie to follow. If the additional $10,000 is financed by a second mortgage at 16% calculated monthly (16.5429% calculated semi-annually) and amortized over 10 years, the total interest cost for the $10,000 loan will be $10,102.12, a savings of almost $13,000, *achieved despite the higher interest rate*.

True, the amortization for the second mortgage is only 10 years and not 25 years. True again that the payment for the second mortgage is $167.51, which is higher than the additional monthly cost for financing the $10,000 through a first mortgage. Most second mortgages, though, are arranged for a specific purpose as pointed out, and borrowers want to retire the loan as soon as possible because it reflects an extra expense in their personal financing. A shorter amortization accomplishes this very purpose, and makes a second mortgage an attractive alternative. Structured in this fashion, the second mortgage option allows Ian and Marie to reduce their indebtedness faster, and at an overall cost lower than by refinancing the first mortgage.

Borrowers fortunate enough to have low interest rate first mortgages would be wise to consider the second mortgage option as well. This way they can avoid paying off and losing the benefit of the low interest rate first mortgage on a refinancing. The annual interest rate of the two mortgages combined could be substantially lower than current rates.

Jeff and Joanne have a $40,000 first mortgage at 11% and need a further $15,000. The rate quoted them for the second mortgage is 16%, while current first mortgage rates are 13½%. To figure out the approximate average interest rate for a first and second mortgage, take the percentage that each loan is of the total, multiple it by the interest rate for that loan and add the total. For example,

First Mortgage: $$\frac{\$40,000}{\$40,000 + \$15,000} \times 11\% = 8\%$$

Second Mortgage: $$\frac{\$15,000}{\$40,000 + \$15,000} \times 16\% = 4.363\%$$

Total average interest rate: 12.363%. Jeff and Joanne should take the 16% second mortgage and the average interest rate.

If a second mortgage is arranged, several things must be kept in mind. First, the term of the second mortgage should mature at the same time as the existing first mortgage. This gives the borrower maximum flexibility, since the two mortgages could be refinanced as a package or separately, depending upon whichever route is cheaper at that time. If that is not possible, the second mortgage should contain a postponement clause, permitting the existing first mortgage to be renewed or replaced without any difficulty. Otherwise, the second lender could severely restrict the borrower from doing anything with the first mortgage, unless the second lender is also paid off at that time, or is paid a bonus for remaining second in priority. Of course, this would defeat the intent of the borrower.

Second mortgages also serve a distinct purpose when a buyer is purchasing a home, and will have just under 25% equity. MICC and CMHC mortgage payment insurance fees are charged when the loan is high ratio — over 75% of the appraised value. When the shortfall in equity is small and the covenant is strong, some lenders will recommend that the first mortgage be for only 75% of the appraised value. No MICC or CMHC fees have to be paid in these circumstances because the loan is not high ratio. The shortfall would be made up by having the buyer arrange alternative financing such as an unsecured personal loan or a second mortgage with a short amortization and an even shorter term. Although a higher rate of interest will be charged for this additional money, the expense is more than offset by the substantial savings in not having to pay up to $2^{1}/2\%$ of the entire principal as mortgage payment insurance.

Finally, note that most second mortgages are considered to be personal loans secured by land. As such, they have more liberal prepayment privileges, and may be fully open.

30
Condominium Mortgages

Mortgages on condominium units are very similar to those on conventional residential units. In the early years of condominiums, lenders were reluctant to advance money on this form of security. Most institutional lenders now treat a condominium unit as any other form of property and will grant a mortgage provided the other criteria are adequately satisfied.

Many mortgages on condominiums start as a mortgage registered against the whole project. It covers all units as well as the common elements, and is known as a blanket mortgage (it "blankets" the entire condominium). As units are sold and occupied, the blanket mortgage is broken into mortgages for the individual units. One lender who has financed the entire project holds whatever mortgages are registered after closing. With the passage of time, and subsequent transactions, other lenders will finance individual units as in any subdivision.

Several important distinctions between mortgages on condominiums and other types of residential real estate should be noted. Some of these clauses also appear in provincial *Condominium Acts.*

- Borrowers must give their lenders the right to exercise the borrower's vote at meetings of the Condominium Corporation. Lenders require this protection in order to take over complete management of a condominium corporation that is facing a financial crisis. While the ability of a lender to control the vote at a meeting of the condominium corporation diminishes substantially when a large number of different lenders hold unit mortgages, it still enables a lender, either individually or collectively, to protect his investment in the property. Usually the vote is not exercised, but the power to do so remains.

- Borrowers are obligated to give to the lender a copy of all relevant notices and documents within a very short period of time. Notices of any breaches that the borrower becomes aware of, by either the condominium corporation or the unit owners, must also be given to the lender. Again, this is part of the lender's desire to know what is going on in the condominium.

- Borrowers must agree in the mortgage that they will pay punctually all money due to the condominium corporation, such as for common expenses, and to provide proof of payment upon request. In the event of default, the lender can pay the expenses and add them to the mortgage debt. Lenders insist on this, as up to three months' unpaid common expenses, like taxes, will rank higher than a first mortgage.

- Borrowers must agree to comply with, observe and perform all duties and obligations imposed by the *Condominium Act*, the declaration, by-laws, rules and regulations of the condominium corporation, present and future.

Condominium owners must be keenly aware of these clauses, for the consequences of noncompliance are grave indeed. Failure to comply with any of these clauses allows the lender, *at its option*, to demand that the outstanding principal be paid forthwith. In other words, nonpayment of maintenance or violation of the rules and regulations dealing with the keeping of pets on the premises not only would constitute default under the mortgage, but also would allow a lender to "call-in" the mortgage. As harsh as this may seem, those are the rules of the game.

31

Mortgage Miscellany

Post-Dated Cheques/Pre-Authorized Chequing

Many lenders insist that post-dated cheques be delivered to them annually. Others require as a term of the mortgage that the borrower participate in the lender's pre-authorized chequing scheme. Not everyone likes having lenders dipping into his or her bank account monthly, without a signed cheque being issued. The possibility for error is too great.

Find out what a potential lender will require before signing a mortgage commitment. Noncompliance with this clause means default under the mortgage, and a possible "call-in" of the loan.

Also note that some lenders insist that bank accounts be maintained with them, from which the mortgage payments are processed.

Co-Signers

Legally known as guarantors, co-signers offer additional security to a lender. In situations where borrowers are borderline in meeting the income requirements of the lender, a guarantor might help in getting approval for the loan.

A guarantor is obligated to make all payments due the lender and perform all other obligations of the borrower upon default. Usually, if a guarantor is needed for a loan, it is an obvious sign of financial fragility, an exception being a husband guaranteeing a loan to his wife on the matrimonial home. Use of a guarantor, as beneficial as it may seem, could be the first step towards a financial catastrophe. Try to avoid using a guarantor unless it is absolutely necessary.

Avoid Interest-Only Loans

Some lenders will offer "interest-only loans" to borrowers, arguing that the loan is cheaper to borrowers in the long run. *Not so! Stay away from interest-only loans.* They can only do the borrower more harm than good!

Interest on these loans is generally payable monthly, and is usually calculated monthly as well. Lenders do this because it is the easiest way to calculate the interest. While a $50,000 mortgage at 13% calculated *semi-annually* amortized over 25 years costs $551.20 each month, a $50,000 interest-only mortgage calculated *monthly* will cost $541.66 monthly. The savings are under $10 a month, yet no money — absolutely no money — is going towards the principal on an interest-only mortgage. In fact, a $50,000 mortgage at 13% calculated semi-annually amortized over 30 years would cost only $539.89 monthly — less than the interest-only loan — and would be paid off in 30 years by comparison.

Avoid interest-only loans like the plague. Take a blended payment mortgage home.

Statements of Disclosure

With the most recent changes to the *Bank Act*, banks are now obligated to provide to borrowers a Statement of Disclosure *before* the loan is completed. It contains the "highlights" of the mortgage transaction, such as the principal, the interest rate, how it is calculated, the payment, the prepayment privilege, and what will be outstanding on the maturity of the loan, assuming no late payments and no prepayments. Other financial institutions and private lenders are not obligated to provide such a statement to their borrowers.

As helpful as the statements are, they do not provide the one piece of information that all borrowers want to have — how the blended payments made are divided between principal and interest. Only an amortization schedule can provide this, but lenders are not obligated to provide one to their borrowers. Every borrower on a blended mortgage should have an amortization schedule, for how else can the outstanding balance on a mortgage at maturity, or the exact amount of a prepayment, be verified?

Statements of Disclosure, written in every-day English, go a long way towards ensuring borrowers are fully aware of the terms of their mortgage. Their use should be extended. The delivery of amortization schedules to borrowers by lenders, however, would be a welcome move as well.

Mortgage Commitments

Just as lawyers are being asked more and more to review offers to purchase before they are signed, so too with mortgage commitments. To ensure that the mortgage application, mortgage approval and statement of disclosure contain what they are supposed to contain, with no hidden "zingers" and nothing omitted, an increasing number of borrowers are asking their lawyers to review these documents before they are signed. Since most residential mortgage commitments can be reviewed in a very short time, the cost to the borrower to have a lawyer review these documents is money well spent. It also provides sound peace of mind. It makes no sense for a $100,000 offer to have a legal seal of approval if the borrower does not take the same precautions when signing the document to finance $75,000 of that purchase. Home buyers and home owners, when refinancing, cannot afford to be penny wise and pound foolish. Again, while there may be some resistance from the lender about taking the mortgage document to a lawyer, the borrower should be persistent — it's his money, and his home.

32

Mortgage Insurance — Part One

No other term in mortgage financing has more different meanings and has led to so much confusion. Four different situations are covered by "mortgage insurance":

- Fire Insurance
- Term Life Insurance
- Payment Insurance
- Rate Insurance

Unfortunately, because all four types are closely associated with mortgage financing, all four have been referred to at some point as "mortgage insurance." In this chapter, the first type of insurance will be discussed. The other three will be discussed in the next chapter.

Fire Insurance

Most people would arrange insurance on their homes, even if they did not have to, to protect the home and the personal property in it against loss or damage by fire or theft. Personal liability coverage also should be arranged, but that is a different topic altogether. A basic fire insurance policy will protect the dwelling and personal property against loss or damage by fire and specified "extended perils." These include explosions, falling objects, vehicular impact, lightning, riot, vandalism, windstorm and smoke damage. A home owner's package will go further, and provide personal liability as well as coverage against theft.

Where a property has been financed with a mortgage, the lender will want to be shown as having an insurable interest in the property. This means a home buyer should contact his insurance agent and ask that the lender be shown in the loss payable clause as first mortgagee. The borrower's lawyer usually attends to this on a refinancing. When the mortgage is paid off, the loss payable clause will be amended to delete the lender's interest. In this way, if the premises are damaged, but not repaired, the lender can hold sufficient funds from the insurance proceeds to cover the outstanding indebtedness as substituted security.

Few insurance policies are fully prepared and issued prior to closing, although they are effective as of that time. To satisfy lenders, insurance agents will issue "binder letters" indicating that on the borrower's behalf they have "bound" (arranged) insurance with an insurance company for a specified amount, effective the day of closing, stating the expiry date and to whom loss payable should be made as first mortgagee. The borrower should arrange to have the binder letter in his lawyer's hands as early as possible before closing, so that the lawyer in turn can deliver it to the lender for approval. Most lenders will close on the basis of the binder letter, although they do want the policy to be delivered to them as soon as possible after closing.

When a mortgage is refinanced, the name of the old lender must be removed from the loss payable clause, and the name of the new lender be inserted. This is usually carried out by the borrower's lawyer.

The amount of insurance coverage for a property should be determined independently of the amount of the outstanding mortgage. The key element is the full insurable value of the building. Most mortgages require that insurance be arranged on this basis. Prudent borrowers will do this, whether or not they have a mortgage, because it provides the greatest possible amount of insurance coverage — the value of the building as determined for insurance purposes. Coverage should also be on a replacement cost basis in order to cover the cost of rebuilding the dwelling at current prices. In this way, no reduction need be made for depreciation. While an additional premium is charged for full replacement cost coverage, only in this way can a home owner replace his building with one of similar type and quality without having to take depreciation into account.

When deciding how much insurance to arrange, remember that the land does not need to be insured. Even if the dwelling were to be totally destroyed in a fire, the land does not burn and is still available to be rebuilt upon. If the lender has had the property appraised, information should be available as to the value of the land and the replacement cost value of the building. Obtain this information from the lender before making arrangements with an insurance agent. It will help to determine the necessary amount of coverage.

Some mortgages demand further that insurance coverage must be maintained for the full amount of the mortgage, even if this amount exceeds the full insurable value of the property. Clauses like these cause headaches for borrowers.

Phil and Lori are buying a property for $100,000. The lot is worth $30,000, and the full insurable value of the house is $70,000. If they arrange a $60,000 mortgage, the lender will require at least $60,000 worth of insurance coverage to cover the full amount of the mortgage. Being prudent, Phil and Lori plan to arrange $70,000 worth of insurance coverage to fully insure the house value.

Jason and Mandy are buying a similar $100,000 house, but are financing it with a $75,000 mortgage. Now the dilemma arises. The full insurable value of the dwelling is only $70,000. Any excess insurance coverage is really being wasted, because all that is being insured for the extra $5,000 is the land. Nevertheless, some lenders adamantly refuse to advance the mortgage proceeds until they are given proof that $75,000 insurance coverage has been arranged, with loss payable to them as first mortgagee, covering the full amount of the mortgage.

When this happens, borrowers have little alternative but to provide the extra $5,000 insurance coverage, as unnecessary as it may be. Of small consolation to buyers is the fact that the difference in premiums between $70,000 coverage and $75,000 coverage is small — usually so small that it is not worth getting sick over.

Most lenders require that the insurance policy have attached to it either their own insurance clause, or the Standard Mortgage Clause approved by the Insurance Bureau of Canada. This is important to lenders for it provides for the insurance proceeds to be paid directly to lenders in the event of a loss, despite the lack of a direct contractual link between lender and insurer. It also provides an acknowledgment by the insurer that the policy will not be cancelled without notice to the lender. Finally, it provides that the policy is not invalidated despite any intervening act of the borrower. Most insurance policies now contain the IBC Standard Mortgage Clause as a matter of course.

Years ago, most insurance policies were arranged for one to three years, and were assignable to new buyers of the property. The recent trend has been to have insurance policies of only one year on residential dwellings, nonassignable as well. Home buyers should not expect the seller's insurance to be transferred to them on closing, unless a newly constructed home is being purchased. Each buyer has to arrange his own insurance, so buyers should start shopping around early, comparing quotes and coverage, to get the required amount of coverage on the best possible terms. Make sure the insurance coverage takes effect from 12:01 A.M. the date of closing.

33

Mortgage Insurance — Part Two

In the last chapter, fire insurance as a form of mortgage insurance was examined. The three other types of insurance that fall under the same general heading are explored below.

Life Insurance

Life insurance agents sell declining-balance term insurance to borrowers under the heading "Mortgage Insurance." This type of insurance provides a fund from which the mortgage debt will be retired in full if the borrower dies during the term of the loan. Some lenders offer this type of insurance as an option at a nominal fee, but few absolutely require it. Borrowers should carefully analyze the amount of life insurance they have and assess whether or nor it is adequate before deciding whether to purchase this type of insurance.

The insurance is arranged on a declining balance basis; therefore, the insurance coverage is reduced as the outstanding principal is reduced. Once the principal is paid off, this term insurance coverage ends as well.

If a substantial prepayment is made, be sure to ask the lender to reduce the premium being paid for the term life coverage. After all, with less money being outstanding, less money has to be insured — at a supposed lesser cost. If the borrower dies, the insurance would only pay the amount of principal still outstanding, even though the premium had been paid for a larger amount of coverage. Depending on the lender, the insurance premium may be reduced at the borrower's request. Don't expect a reduction in premiums to be made automatically when a prepayment is made. For new loans, find out in writing from the lender *before booking the insurance* how to reduce the insurance premium following a sizable prepayment of principal.

Payment Insurance

Earlier on, when discussing high-ratio mortgages (those for more than 75% of the appraised value of the property), the need for payment insurance was raised. The one-time premium paid by the borrower to a company like the Mortgage Insurance Company of Canada or Canada Mortgage and Housing Corporation could be as high as 2.5% of the total principal amount of the mortgage, and not just the portion over 75% which is high ratio. Also called creditor insurance, it eliminates the risk to lenders of high-ratio loans by guaranteeing payment of the mortgage in the event of default by the borrower. On a $60,000 loan, a borrower would have to pay a premium well over $1000 to ensure a lender that he will honor his financial commitment. While the amount could be paid "up front" on closing, the usual situation is to add it to the outstanding principal, and pay it off monthly in this fashion.

Unless it is absolutely necessary, avoid this type of insurance. It is very expensive. Explore the possibility of a second mortgage for the high-ratio portion as an alternative (see chapter 29).

Interest Rate Insurance

In the February, 1984 Federal Budget, the Mortgage Rate Protection Plan was introduced to protect home owners against sharp rises in interest rates. The plan applies equally to new and renewed mortgages, but not to vendor-take-back or second mortgages. A one-time premium of 1.5% of the outstanding principal is paid to Canada Mortgage and Housing Corporation for this coverage. Again, either it is paid upfront or it is added to the outstanding principal. Mortgages up to $70,000 with terms to maturity of one year or more are protected, the maximum premium being $1,050.

The insurance coverage does not begin until the original term runs out, and provides interest rate protection for the identical period of time. In other words, if a borrower is about to arrange a three-year mortgage, he arranges interest rate protection now, to take effect at the end of the three-year term, to cover the next three-year period. No rate protection is provided for the first 2% increase in interest rates — that remains the borrower's responsibility (the "2% deductible"). If the interest rate on the renewal term is anywhere from 2% to 10% higher than the interest rate for the original mortgage term, 75% of the increase after the 2% deductible is reimbursed to the borrower by the plan. Rate increases of more than 10 percentage points remain the borrower's responsibility.

The drawbacks are obvious. The extremely high cost of coverage is charged at a time when most borrowers cannot afford this type of expense. The 2% deductible is quite sizable, as well. Who knows what interest rates will be when the mortgage matures? If the rate is the same, or less, or only up to 2% higher, no coverage is available, and the money spent for the insurance will have been wasted. If the rate goes up by more than 2%, you the borrower still pick up 25% of the increase. The chart shows what the insurance will pay, and what you will pay.

Amount of Increase	Amount of Increase that Will Be Paid
1%	Nothing
2%	Nothing
3%	.75%
4%	1.5%
5%	2.25%
6%	3.0%
7%	3.75%
8%	4.5%
9%	5.25%
10%	6.0%

Yet the most serious problem is in the implementation of the scheme. The premiums quoted are not pro-rated for mortgage terms shorter than five years. Because of this, there is little advantage in paying the premium for any shorter period of coverage. Yet not all borrowers are prepared to make a commitment for a five-year mortgage, especially when a sizable penalty might have to be paid to break the mortgage.

The benefit of the insurance coverage is transferable to any new owner of the property. The mortgage is insured against increases in interest rates, not the borrower.

34

Interest Buy-Downs

Buying down the interest rate (or discounting a mortgage) is a very common marketing tool used by builders of new homes. This enables them to offer lower than market interest rates to purchasers/borrowers to encourage the purchase of their homes. Builders often emphasize the lower than market interest rate as they do lot size, a paved driveway and central air-conditioning. Borrowers must know how an interest buy-down works, what it does and does not accomplish and the problems it can cause before deciding whether to commit to such a loan.

In this world, no one gets anything for nothing. So too with buy-downs. There are costs associated with them, usually substantial. Who should bear the costs? It will certainly not be the lender, who wants current interest rates, plain and simple. Instead, the builder initially bears the costs, who in turn passes them on to the buyer.

Buy-downs are simply an application of the old principle — "you can pay me now or you can pay me later." If current interest rates are 13%, lenders want to receive 13%, not the 8% that the builder wants a purchaser to pay. The solution rests with the interest buy-down, where the builder applies the principle of present value interest differentials, discussed in chapter 12.

Ready Construction has just completed negotiating its mortgage commitment with its lender, Vaughan Trust. The interest rate to be paid by purchasers of Ready Construction homes is 8% for three years, amortized over 25 years. Current interest rates are 13%. If Ralph and Alice need a $50,000 mortgage, then Ready Construction must prepay up-front the present value of the interest differential. The principle is exactly the same when a borrower wishes to prepay a mortgage in full before its maturity and interest rates have fallen. The present value of the 5% differential for the three-year term of the mortgage is $5,841.38. This is the amount that the builder, Ready Construction, must pay to the lender, Vaughan Trust, to "buy-down" this mortgage. The lender is still receiving 13%, but it is being paid differently. Instead of 13% interest being paid over the next three years, an 8% return will be paid over that period, the difference being made up from the "up-front" money and the interest it will generate over the next three years. The lender is in exactly the same position either way after three years have passed.

How does the builder recoup this money? By adding it to the selling price, that's how! With an interest buy-down, builders can offer very low interest rate loans to their buyers. Even interest-free loans are possible. For example, a one-year interest-free loan of $10,000 when interest rates are 13% will cost a builder only $1,183.41.

While borrowers may think they save substantially from interest buy-downs, they really do not. In fact, they can cause more headaches in the future than problems they solve today. Builders add the interest buy-down to the purchase price of the house, so buyers need to assume a larger mortgage on closing. While the monthly mortgage expense becomes more manageable with an interest buy-down, the purchase price and the outstanding principal on the mortgage assumed will be higher. Without an interest buy-down, the monthly mortgage payments would be higher due to the higher interest rate, but the purchase price and the outstanding mortgage would be lower. It's six of one, half a dozen of the other.

Ready Construction was selling houses for $70,000, requiring $20,000 down and offering $50,000 mortgages at 13% with monthly payments of $551.20. There were just a few buyers. After arranging an interest buy-down to 8% for three years, at a cost of $5,841.38, Ready Construction upped house prices to $76,000. While $20,000 down was still required, the cost of carrying the $56,000 mortgage offered at 8% was $427.40. Buyers flocked to the sales trailer. The subdivision sold out in a short time!

The lender did not suffer from the interest buy-down, nor did the builder, who sold his homes faster, at no additional cost. All the expense of the buy-down was borne by the buyer, and the buyer *alone*.

Interest buy-downs can be dangerous for the unwary. Look at the dilemma that Ralph and Alice face, who bought a Ready Construction home with the $56,000 mortgage at 8%. After three years' payments on this mortgage, they owe $53,566.93. Interest rates at renewal are 13%, and now the benefit of the lower than normal interest rate mortgage is gone. After three years, they now face a monthly payment of $590.52, an increase of over 38%, which they find impossible to handle. Only with parental assistance are they able to avoid losing the house. The low interest rate arising from the buy-down did not encourage them to buy the house — it enticed them — and almost caused their financial downfall.

To reduce the likelihood that problems like this will

arise, purchasers/borrowers who are assuming builder mortgages below current interest rates should ensure they would still qualify for the mortgage, even if it were booked at current interest rates. Many lenders do this when approving borrowers in buy-down situations in any event. While no one can predict the future, such advance planning can go a long way in protecting borrowers, their homes, their investments and their reputations.

Interest buy-downs are not entirely limited to new home situations. When interest rates were extremely high in 1981 and 1982, many sellers of resale homes used interest buy-downs as a marketing tool to sell their properties when mortgage rates were 20% and higher. A clause was inserted into the offer to the effect that the buyer would arrange a mortgage on specified terms (i.e., $50,000 amortized over 25 years with interest at 16%). The present value interest differential would be paid by the seller in a lump sum to the lender. This enabled buyers to pay a lower than market interest rate, making the mortgage payment more manageable while giving the lender the current interest rate. Of course, the cost borne by the seller would be added to the selling price of the house. While not as popular in times of lower interest rates, the idea can always be used in appropriate circumstances.

Home owners refinancing their mortgages, and even buyers acquiring a home, can employ the same principle to make mortgage payments more manageable. Here, the only person available to bear the cost of the interest buy-down is the borrower. David and Estee have been offered an interest rate of 16% on the renewal of their $50,000 mortgage, amortized over 25 years with payments of $659.53. To make their mortgage payments more manageable, they decided to buy-down the mortgage for one year, to 13%. The total cost to David and Estee, which must be paid up-front when the mortgage is renewed, is $1,299.70. Effectively, they are still paying 16% on their mortgage to the lender. Some of the interest is being paid now as a lump-sum payment, and some over the course of the next year. The monthly payment indeed is much easier to handle ($551.20) as a result.

To help calculate the approximate amount of an interest buy-down or mortgage discount, consult a "Mortgage Value Table" which is available in the reference section of most municipal libraries. It shows the price to be paid per $1,000 of outstanding mortgage to produce the required interest rate. Two sample pages are shown below.

For loans amortized over 25 years, an interest buy-down from 13% to 8% will cost Ready Construction $117 per $1,000 of mortgage. To determine this, note that the value of a mortgage discounted from 13% to 8% amortized over 25 years and having a three-year term is $883 per $1,000. As the size of the mortgage to be discounted is $50,000, the approximate cost to Ready Construction for the mortgage discount is $117 times 50, or $5,850. This is quite close to the exact calculation of $5,841.38 referred to earlier. In David and Estee's case, the value of the mortgage after the interest buy-down occurs is $974 per $1,000, or $48,700 for a $50,000 mortgage. The approximate discount or buy-down: $1,300, almost exactly what was calculated earlier ($1,299.70).

Interest buy-downs do save borrowers some money, but there is a cost involved, usually borne by the borrower. If anything, interest buy-downs actually accomplish little more than shifting the time when the interest will be paid to the lender. Serious problems lurk behind the apparent glossy benefits for the unwary. Make sure you fully understand how interest buy-downs work before putting pen to paper for such a loan.

MORTGAGE VALUE TABLE
SHOWING PRICE TO BE PAID PER $1000 OUTSTANDING

	8.00%								25		
	MORTGAGE RATE					YEARS AMORTIZED					
I					TERM IN YEARS						I
Yield	1	2	3	4	5	6	7	8	9	10	Yield
9.0	991	983	975	968	962	957	952	948	944	941	9.0
9.5	986	974	963	953	944	936	929	923	917	913	9.5
10.0	982	966	951	938	927	916	907	899	892	886	10.0
10.5	977	957	939	923	909	897	886	876	868	860	10.5
11.0	973	949	928	909	892	878	865	854	844	836	11.0
11.5	969	941	916	895	876	859	845	832	821	812	11.5
12.0	964	933	905	881	860	841	825	812	800	789	12.0
12.5	960	925	894	867	844	824	807	792	779	767	12.5
13.0	955	917	883	854	829	807	788	772	758	747	13.0
13.5	951	909	872	841	814	791	771	753	739	726	13.5
14.0	947	901	862	828	799	774	753	735	720	707	14.0
14.5	943	894	852	816	785	759	737	718	702	689	14.5
15.0	939	886	841	803	771	744	721	701	685	671	15.0
15.5	934	879	831	791	757	729	705	685	668	654	15.5
16.0	930	871	821	779	744	714	690	669	651	637	16.0

	13.00%						25			
	MORTGAGE RATE						YEARS AMORTIZED			
I				TERM IN YEARS						I
Yield	1	2	3	4	5	6	7	8	9	10	Yield

I Yield	1	2	3	4	5	6	7	8	9	10	I Yield
14.0	991	984	977	971	966	962	958	955	952	950	14.0
14.5	987	976	966	957	950	944	938	934	930	927	14.5
15.0	983	968	955	944	934	926	919	913	908	904	15.0
15.5	978	960	944	930	919	909	900	893	887	882	15.5
16.0	**974**	952	933	917	903	892	882	874	867	861	16.0
16.5	970	944	922	904	889	875	864	855	847	841	16.5
17.0	966	937	912	891	874	859	847	837	828	821	17.0
17.5	961	929	902	879	860	844	830	819	810	802	17.5
18.0	957	922	892	867	846	829	814	802	792	784	18.0
18.5	953	914	882	855	832	814	799	786	775	767	18.5
19.0	949	907	872	843	819	799	783	770	759	750	19.0
19.5	945	900	862	831	806	785	768	754	743	734	19.5
20.0	941	892	853	820	793	772	754	739	728	718	20.0
20.5	937	885	843	809	781	758	740	725	713	703	20.5
21.0	933	878	834	798	769	745	726	711	698	688	21.0

35

Holding A Mortgage Through One's Own RRSP

Sounds strange doesn't it? Being both lender and borrower at the same time? Can Arthur borrow funds from his own self-administered Registered Retirement Savings Plan, secured by a mortgage on his own house? Yes, he can! This type of arrangement is now permitted in Canada, and has distinct benefits.

Instead of having money tied up in an RRSP, the funds can be withdrawn from the plan in this manner and used without having to "crash" or terminate the plan. If the money is used for business or investment purposes, the interest paid is a deductible expense for income tax purposes. The interest earned by the RRSP is tax-free income to the plan, no matter for what purpose the funds are used. Both first and second mortgages are permitted. Finally, the borrowers should be able to get extremely beneficial mortgage terms — "fully open" for example — if the lender is not too demanding!

Certain important restrictions do exist on borrowing from one's own RRSP. The plan is only available through NHA approved lenders (most major financial institutions) and requires that the borrower have a self-administered RRSP. The mortgage rates and terms must be similar to those in the marketplace. Extra expenses are involved as well, since the mortgage must be insured by CMHC or MICC. Depending on the size of the mortgage and the amount of equity behind it, the insurance could cost up to $2^1/2\%$ of the principal amount. Fees will have to be paid, both "set-up charges" for the transaction as well as annual administrative fees. These could run into the hundreds of dollars annually. The costs normally associated with mortgage loans such as appraisal fees, legal fees and disbursements would also be incurred.

Another option which would help reduce the costs involved in using an RRSP as a mortgage investment vehicle is for two friends to loan money to each other from their respective RRSPs. Bert and Ernie, for example, are lodge brothers and have known each other for years. Bert has agreed to loan $25,000 from his own RRSP to Ernie and vice versa, all other terms including the interest rate (identical on each loan) being comparable to those in the marketplace. With the mortgage funds being lent to a non-arm's-length (i.e., non-related) third party, the mortgage insurance fee is totally eliminated. Since the costs of insurance for a mortgage on their own properties would have been prohibitive, each of Bert and Ernie feel very comfortable with this arrangement. It permits them to do something they otherwise could not have afforded to do.

Obviously, holding a mortgage on one's own property through an RRSP is not for everyone. The appropriate circumstances also must exist to have cross-plans in effect. Nevertheless, using a self-administered RRSP to hold a mortgage is an interesting option to keep in mind for future reference, if the circumstances warrant it.

36

What To Do When Your Mortgage Reaches Maturity

This chapter deals with the concerns of current home owners who must renew their mortgage. Home buyers will also find it of interest, for they will eventually find themselves in the same situation.

Many borrowers become anxious when they know their mortgage is maturing in the near future. Uncertainty over interest rates is probably the most significant reason for this anxiety. Too often borrowers will accept new terms offered by their lenders — as if relieved the mortgage is "safe" — without shopping around.

While the maturity of a mortgage is a "day of reckoning," when key decisions must be made, the maturity of a mortgage does offer three important benefits to borrowers: (1) It forces home owners to take stock of themselves, to analyze their financial picture and to set goals for the future — both short term and long range. This intensive self-analysis is essential if the right decisions are to be made; (2) It allows borrowers to prepay as much money as they wish, without any interest penalty whatsoever. That's right — no interest penalties. Even the most watertight closed mortgage opens up fully on its maturity; (3) It gives borrowers an opportunity to restructure their affairs, to take advantage of some of the new developments in the area of mortgage financing, all with a view to reducing the extremely high interest costs associated with mortgage financing. In short, is the existing mortgage still suitable?

A common misconception must be put to bed at this time. Lenders are under no obligation to renew a mortgage on its maturity, unless the mortgage specifically provides for it. Despite this, most institutional lenders do offer to renew mortgages on their maturity. Individual lenders are a different story. Unless the lender carries on business as a money lender, most individuals and, in particular, vendors who took back mortgages on the sale of their property, will not offer to renew the mortgage. Borrowers who have been persistently late in making their mortgage payments, or whose properties have fallen substantially in value with a resulting loss of equity, may find institutional lenders reluctant to renew their mortgages. However, if a lender has a well secured property with a good covenant, and if the borrower on the renewal is prepared to pay current rates, lenders generally will not look elsewhere for a source to place their funds.

Upon maturity of a mortgage, the borrower must choose from one of the three "R's" — (1) retire the loan, (2) refinance the property with another lender, or (3) renew with the existing lender.

Retiring the loan is easy. Simply pay the money owing to the lender together with the discharge fee of approximately $100, register the discharge, notify the insurance company that the loan is paid off in order to remove the lender's name from the loss payable clause in the insurance policy and *voila* — it's mortgage burning time.

If the loan is not to be paid off in full, then the borrower can stay with Peter, or borrow from Peter to pay off Paul. In either case, borrowers should take advantage of the fact the mortgage is due and payable and that the terms of the mortgage must be recast to best suit them. While most of the earlier commentary applied equally to renewals and refinancings, several specific comments are in order.

- Renewing with the same lender is considerably cheaper than refinancing. Since refinancing involves arranging a new loan with a new lender, all those costs associated with a new mortgage loan must be incurred. These include appraisal, arranging, possibly a new survey, interest to the interest adjustment date, legal fees and disbursements, discharge fees and so on. Minimum cost? — at least $500, probably considerably more. Renewing involves signing a contract, setting out the new terms and conditions, while reaffirming all the other terms. Cost: usually under $100. While most lenders do not register renewal agreements on title (an internal policy decision, since the changes to the mortgage should be on title), expect to pay at least an additional $50 if registration is required. Remember, though, that private lenders and especially vendor-take-back lenders are less likely to renew a mortgage than financial institutions.
- Be absolutely certain that the amortization period for the renewal/replacement term is reduced to take into account the number of years that payments have already been made. The new amortization should not exceed the amortization *remaining* on the old loan. Arnie and Hyla have a three-year term/25-year amortization mortgage which is coming up for renewal

shortly. The amortization on the renewal or refinancing should not exceed 22 years, assuming no prepayments have been made, because three years' worth of payments towards the 25-year amortized life of the mortgage have already been made. If prepayments have been made, the amortization should not exceed the remaining amortization after taking the prepayments into account. Therefore, if the prepayments reduced the amortization by four years, the renewal or refinanced mortgage should have an amortization not exceeding 18 years (25 less three less four). If a 25-year amortized mortgage is arranged, a slightly lower payment will be made monthly, but Arnie and Hyla will be in debt for 25 more years, not just eighteen. This means that the total interest costs will be higher as well. Going back to a 25-year amortization in this situation will mean that Arnie and Hyla will feel as if they are perpetually behind the eight ball. If the lender will not provide the precise amortization being sought (although there is no cogent reason why lenders should not do this), then round down the amortization, not up, despite the slightly higher payment that will result. If their lender refuses to offer an 18-year amortized mortgage, Arnie and Hyla should opt for a 15-year amortization, rather than a 20-year amortization. The additional cost per month is more than offset by the five mortgage-free years that will result.

- Since the contract has matured, there is no obligation to renew or replace the mortgage for the same outstanding principal. If more money is needed than was outstanding previously, such as to retire a second mortgage, then a new mortgage document will have to be registered to reflect the higher principal. Of course, borrowers can prepay any amount at maturity that they wish, without incurring any penalty. Besides changing the principal, borrowers can change the term of the mortgage as well as the amortization period for the loan. Maturity is an excellent time for borrowers to select the appropriate payment they wish to make in the future. Even the lender can be changed, if the borrower wishes to refinance the loan and not simply renew it. Changes in interest rates will be determined by the lender and not the borrower, but all other factors should be decided by the borrower after careful thought. Some lenders may offer several different mortgage terms with the interest rate varying accordingly.

- When a prepayment is made in the midst of a mortgage term, the payment stays the same and the amortization is reduced. When additional funds are paid towards a mortgage on its maturity, whether on a renewal or refinancing, one of two things can happen:

    i) the same payment is maintained and the amortization alone is reduced. This is the same as a prepayment before maturity; or
    ii) the same amortization can be maintained, and the payment is reduced. This is an important option when borrowers face a substantially increased payment due to rising interest costs.

Tom and Geraldine, and Neil and Jane, have $50,000 mortgages amortized over 25 years. In Tom and Geraldine's case, the interest rate is 13% with monthly payments of $551.20. After one year, they owe $49,699.18. Facing renewal at the same rate, they wish to prepay $1,000 towards the mortgage. If the prepayment is applied to reduce the amortization, the payment for the renewed term will stay at $551.20 and the amortization will be reduced to 21.42 years from 24 years, saving $16,422.07 in interest. If the prepayment is applied to reduce the payment, the amortization will stay at 24 years and the payment will be reduced to $540.11, saving $2,195.43.

In Neil and Jane's case, the interest rate has risen from 13% to 19%. Without a prepayment, the new monthly payment will be $767.29. By prepaying $1,000 to reduce the amortization of the mortgage, their new amortization will be 18.85 years while the mortgage payment remains at $767.29, saving $46,463.72. On the other hand, if $1,000 is applied to reduce the monthly payment, the amortization on Neil and Jane's loan will remain at 24 years, while the payment will fall to $751.85, saving $3,440.27.

Applying the prepayment to reduce the amortization results in large savings to borrowers. For those home owners who cannot handle tremendous increases in the monthly payment because of high mortgage rates, a prepayment will help make the monthly payment a little more manageable.

- If interest rates are lower on the renewal/refinancing than was the case during the original term, borrowers should consider choosing the largest payment they can handle in the range between the "old payment" and the "new payment." Larry and Maureen originally had a $50,000 one-year mortgage at 19% amortized over 25 years. The payments were $770.28. On renewal/refinancing, the rate for the $49,892.33 outstanding was reduced to 13%. A pleasant surprise indeed! If they did nothing and renewed the mortgage for a 24-year amortization, the payment would have fallen to $553.35. On analyzing their situation more closely, Larry and Maureen realized that they could afford to pay more than the minimum payment every month. Having learned to keep the belt tight the previous year, they did not want to automatically accept the new, lower monthly payment. They wanted to loosen the belt slightly, but not all the way.

Instead, they opted for middle ground — a payment of $675.00 instead of $553.35. What a surprise! Instead of the amortization being 24 years, it was reduced to just over 12 years. If they had kept the payment exactly the same as the previous year (i.e., $770.28), the amortization would have been reduced to just over nine years. With a monthly payment of $675, the interest cost was reduced by over $62,000!

Institutional lenders might balk at choosing an odd amortization based on a nice round payment. Private lenders generally do not show such resistance. Banks and trust companies prefer to choose an odd payment based on a nice round amortization, as strange as it sounds. If absolutely necessary, Larry and Maureen could have chosen a 10-year amortization with payments of $735.01, or a 15-year amortization with payments of $620.18 on the renewal financing, just to suit the lender.

Adoption of this approach, when interest rates have fallen, is another example of POPS — Paying Off the Principal Sooner. Every dollar paid over and above $553.35 each month helps retire the principal sooner. A shorter amortization and lower interest costs result from this.

- Even if the interest rate increases, consider a higher than quoted monthly payment, if possible. The results may be quite manageable, and the benefits of reducing the interest costs could be quite substantial. Howard and Sheila's three-year 13% mortgage comes due soon. Originally booked at $50,000 and amortized over 25 years, the balance outstanding on maturity will be $48,971.01. Although the interest rate has increased to 15%, they would like to increase the payment to $675, reflecting the increases in salary they have received over the last three years. Their lender refused to renew the mortgage with a round payment, saying only round amortizations could be selected. Since a payment of $675 would have produced an amortization of about 14.65 years, they opted for a 15-year amortization on the renewal, with monthly payments of $670.42. The total interest savings: $42,889.99. Again, increasing the payment to reduce the amortization means borrowers benefit from POPS.

- Most lenders notify the borrowers in the last month before maturity, and after the last regular cheque has been cashed, if they are prepared to renew the mortgage and if so on what terms. Some will not set a rate until 15 days or so before maturity. Nevertheless, because the contract is due on maturity, lenders are under no legal obligation to contact borrowers, asking for their money. The onus rests with the borrower. To be prudent, do not wait too long for notice from the lender. If a borrower has not heard from his lender 20 days prior to maturity, he should call the lender, and see what is happening. Never wait until the last minute. Also, be sure to get the dates right. A mortgage closing in mid-September with an interest adjustment date of October 1 will have its first payment due on November 1. Maturity will not be November 1, but October 1. A number of clients have forgotten this, and have had to scurry about *after* maturity, quickly arranging a new loan on whatever terms were presented. Remember, maturity is not based on the first payment date, but is based on the interest adjustment date (which is one month before the first payment date). On the other hand, borrowers seriously thinking of taking their mortgage business to another lender should start making inquiries no later than 60 days before maturity. Days and weeks can be spent by the lender in obtaining the approval and by the lawyer in processing the refinancing. Even those borrowers unsure of whether to refinance or renew their mortgages would be wise to start their comparative shopping early. Deciding which route to follow can be a time-consuming process. Eliminate unnecessary additional anxiety — get going early!

- A number of lenders are now offering "early renewals" to borrowers. To allay the fears of borrowers concerned that interest rates will rise between now and the time their mortgage comes up for renewal, these lenders will permit existing mortgages to be renewed before their maturity at current interest rates. When early renewal can be invoked, the administrative fee charged to borrowers, the manner in which interest differentials are handled and the question of a premium rate for early renewal loans all differ in the financial community. Borrowers who are concerned that interest rates will accompany the next space shuttle can lock in now — for a price, of course.

- Mortgage refinancing should take place the day the old mortgage matures, but this is not always possible. The tardiness of the old lender deciding what he is prepared to do, the slowness of the decision-making process by the new lender, and the time spent by the borrower's lawyer in completing a search of title and other investigations account for these delays. Some borrowers become apprehensive if the old mortgage is not discharged precisely on its maturity date. Take heart, borrowers, all is not lost. According to the *Interest Act of Canada*, no higher rate of interest can be charged on a mortgage after maturity than before, unless by mutual consent. Furthermore, the most popular remedy open to lenders, power of sale, cannot be invoked until the mortgage has been in default for 15 days. The combined effect of these rules is that borrowers can usually "buy" another 15 days on the old mortgage at the old mortgage rate, if necessary, without any adverse consequences. Courtesy, of course, requires that the old lender be notified of the delay, and be assured the new mortgage funds will be advanced shortly. This should be ample time for the refinancing to be completed, if commenced before the old mortgage matures. Even if more time is needed after the 15-day period, it is unlikely the old lender will take proceedings against the borrower if proper assurances are given that the loan will be paid off imminently. While a higher rate of interest could be demanded and enforced if necessary, the cost to the borrower would be nominal. A 5% short-term increase in rates on a $50,000 mortgage would be $6.85 a day. Don't fret! Just ensure the refinancing takes place no later than 15 days after the old mortgage matures.

• No penalty is incurred for prepaying a mortgage on maturity, so this is the ideal time for borrowers to rearrange their affairs and to make mortgage interest deductible, if possible. See chapter 38.

37

What Borrowers Should Do
If They Sell Their House

While borrowers locked in with high interest rate mortgages obviously would like to break their mortgages, the real need to prepay a mortgage in full arises when a property is sold and the purchaser does not wish to take over the mortgage. This could happen for a number of reasons: the outstanding principal is much higher than the buyer needs to assume; the outstanding principal is too low to suit the buyer's needs, or the buyer is getting a company loan or a family mortgage. If the mortgage is fully open (category **A**), the borrower can prepay the loan without any concern. Category **B** mortgages can also be paid off readily, for the mortgage specifies exactly what the prepayment penalty will be. Mortgages falling into categories **C**, **D**, and **E**, which are closed either in part or in whole, pose the greatest problem. Even if the mortgage has limited open privileges, such as 10% with or without a penalty, the question remains: what would the lender charge as a penalty for the remaining 90% of the mortgage? The final decision rests solely with the lender and how he exercises his discretion.

All is not lost. A technique exists, not openly publicized by financial institutions, to deal with this situation in appropriate circumstances. It is called "portability" — taking the old mortgage to a new property being acquired. Since most borrowers when buying a new home need a larger mortgage than they previously had, the mortgage on the new house could be set with an interest rate acknowledging that "old money" (i.e., money secured by the old property) as well as "new money" (the additional money required to purchase the new home) is being borrowed. Instead of paying a large prepayment penalty to cancel the mortgage on the old property, the interest rate on the new mortgage takes all of these factors into account. Of course, the property and the borrower otherwise must qualify for the loan.

Earlier, the plight of Peter and Cathy was discussed. They wanted to prepay a 16% mortgage with two years to run when rates had fallen to 12%. They faced a present value prepayment penalty of $3,295.10. Instead of paying the penalty up-front to discharge the mortgage, and arranging a new mortgage from another lender, they approached their existing lender about taking the old mortgage to their new home. They needed a new first mortgage of $80,000 to buy the other property. As approximately $50,000 was outstanding on the old mortgage, $30,000 new money was needed. By combining five-eighths of a loan at 16% and three-eighths of the loan at 12%, the new two-year mortgage on the new house would cost them 14$\frac{1}{2}$% — *but there was no prepayment penalty.* Peter and Cathy were happy — their cash flow was not devastated by any prepayment penalty. The lender was happy — not only did he keep a customer and a $50,000 loan, but also he was able to put another $30,000 out on the street at current rates, the total mortgage of $80,000 being secured against a much more valuable property. The interest rate and subsequent monthly payment was set blending the old component with the new, stirring together both parts in a pot, to get a figure that was fair to both sides.

Even if no new mortgage money is needed, transporting a mortgage is an effective way to eliminate the prepayment penalty that otherwise would be charged on the sale of the property. Portability also should be of interest to those borrowers selling their homes when the interest rate on the outstanding mortgage is lower than current rates. Instead of the purchaser of that property assuming the below-market interest rate, sellers transporting the mortgage to a new property can keep the old interest rate for themselves. If any additional funds were required, they would be lent at current interest rates. The rate charged then would be a combination of the "old" rate and the "new" rate. Portability of this type is another example of how mortgages these days are increasingly resembling personal loans given to borrowers, tailored to their circumstances, but secured by land.

Advance planning is needed when thinking of transporting a mortgage to another property. The idea is still in its infancy, so be prepared for lender resistance. But be persistent. Transporting a mortgage will mean the prepayment penalty will be substantially reduced, if not totally eliminated. It's worth fighting for.

38

Making Interest Deductible

Everyone knows that interest paid on residential mortgages in Canada is not deductible from income. Everyone knows that American taxpayers can deduct the interest on their home mortgage in determining the amount of tax payable. What everyone did not know (until now) is that there is a way for Canadians in some situations to deduct the interest expense on their mortgage.

The key is for Canadians to arrange their affairs so their house clearly and unequivocally becomes the security for a bona fide loan — one made to generate and earn income. The connection among the loan, the security and the business purpose to which the funds are put must be genuine and unambiguous. Then, the interest expense is deductible.

The reason why the funds were borrowed and where the funds went will determine if the interest is deductible. To be deductible, the borrowed money clearly must have been used to buy a business or make investments. The fact a principal residence is the security for the loan is immaterial if the proper use can be established. Keep in mind that Revenue Canada Taxation is looking for any slip-up or gap in the chain to disallow the deduction. Therefore, it is absolutely essential to leave a proper "paper trail" — to have written legal documents establishing every aspect of the transaction, every step of the way. This is needed to be able to prove in a court of law, if necessary, that the money was used to earn income. In addition, borrowers must be meticulous, painstaking, accurate, fussy, finicky, precise, exact and letter-perfect. Nothing else is good enough.

What is the benefit of making the interest expense tax deductible? Two couples, Sam and Helen, and Rob and Laura, are each in the 33⅓% marginal tax bracket. This means that every additional dollar earned nets them only 66.6 cents, the remainder being payable as tax. Each couple earns $50,000, and has $5,000 in mortgage interest expenses. Sam and Helen are unable to deduct their interest expense, while Rob and Laura can. Sam and Helen, therefore, pay income tax of $16,666.67 (33⅓% of $50,000). Rob and Laura will pay tax of 33⅓% on $45,000 (the $50,000 in income less then $5,000 deductible interest expense). Total tax payable: $15,000. Total savings for Rob and Laura by making the interest deductible: $1,666.67 this year alone!

"Expensive loans" are those arranged for personal purposes, such as buying a house. The interest is not deductible. "Cheap loans" are those arranged to generate business and investment income, where the interest is deductible.

How can borrowers with existing mortgages rearrange their affairs so that the interest on a mortgage registered against their principal residence becomes a tax-deductible expense? Much depends on the borrower's present financial situation. Fred and Wilma have a $50,000 mortgage, and also have $50,000 in "other assets," such as Canada Savings Bonds, Guaranteed Investment Certificates, Term Deposits, and stocks and bonds. If these were liquidated with the funds applied to retire their mortgage, the house would be fully paid off, but the "other assets" would be gone too. (Note that capital gains tax might have to be paid on the sale or redemption of some of these assets.) Fred and Wilma are scratching their heads. They really do not want to get rid of those assets, but they do want a tax-deductible expense. What should they do?

If the original mortgage debt is discharged, all Fred and Wilma have to do is arrange a mortgage and reacquire their former assets *with the borrowed funds*. As the mortgage loan has been arranged specifically for a business and investment reason, to generate and earn income, the interest expense is now deductible from their other income. A time lag should exist between liquidating and reacquiring the assets to prevent having the argument raised that the transactions were a sham. Done properly, Fred and Wilma have converted their nondeductible interest into deductible interest, owning the same net assets as before, after the dust settles.

The tax deduction is so valuable, that often it is worthwhile for borrowers to pay a higher rate of interest on a business loan than was previously paid for a non-business loan. Barney and Betty found this out. Under their old nondeductible $50,000 mortgage at 11%, the annual interest cost was approximately $5,500. Current interest rates of 13% for their "interest deductible" mortgage means an interest cost of about $6,500. Being in the 40% marginal tax bracket, Barney and Betty will save 40% of $6,500 or $2,600 in tax this year by restructuring their affairs. As the additional interest paid totals $1,000, only $1,600 in tax will be saved this year. Much of that will go towards the "one-time" cost of rearranging their affairs. Next year, though, those costs will not have to be incurred again, meaning considerable further savings in tax for Barney and Betty.

These figures assume that no prepayment penalty is incurred on paying off the old loan with the funds from the new loan. Anyone with a fully open mortgage could take advantage of the arrangement immediately. For all other borrowers, any penalty that needs to be paid reduces the effectiveness of the conversion. Yet all mortgages are open on their maturity, without penalty. Maturity of an existing loan, therefore, affords an excellent opportunity to convert a nondeductible mortgage loan into a tax-deductible business expense. Furthermore, as the maturity of the mortgage is a fixed "target date," borrowers can make all the necessary plans and arrangements well in advance, knowing precisely when the wheels must be set in motion. Everything that is properly prearranged (and correctly documented) should fall into place once the existing mortgage matures.

Ted and Mary would like to make their interest deductible, but have only $30,000 worth of "other assets" to apply to their $50,000 mortgage. Maturity takes place in 60 days' time. No problem. What Ted and Mary should do is liquidate their assets as described above, and reduce the existing loan to $20,000. After the appropriate time lag, a new second mortgage is arranged for $30,000. Although technically this loan is a second mortgage, it is virtually as safe as a first mortgage, and would have been part of the first mortgage if the restructuring were not taking place. For that reason that interest rate on that loan should be comparable with the interest rate for the first mortgage. The $30,000 from the new second mortgage then is used to reacquire the "other assets." In this fashion, the interest on the

$30,000 second mortgage becomes deductible, while the interest on the $20,000 remaining on the first mortgage is not. Both mortgages should mature at the same time, so the exercise then can be repeated, if desired, to make the entire mortgage a deductible business loan.

Obviously, some costs will be incurred in rearranging one's affairs. Legal fees and other charges will be incurred on the new mortgage. A prepayment penalty may have to be incurred to discharge the old loan. The rate of interest on the new mortgage may exceed that of the old loan. Therefore, as beneficial as the concept sounds, it is not for the small investor or the home owner with only a few thousand dollars in Canada Savings Bonds or Guaranteed Investment Certificates. To be worthwhile, the amount of the existing "other assets" should closely match the amount of the outstanding mortgage. In any event, proper professional guidance from a lawyer and an accountant are absolutely essential. This is not the type of an arrangement where taxpayers can afford to fly solo. Yet in the proper circumstances, Canadians who do not take advantage of this arrangement are shortchanging themselves.

39

What Do I Do: Long Term Or Short Term?

Deciding whether to go short term or long term on a mortgage is one of the toughest decisions to make. Obviously, it is important to tailor the term and other terms of the mortgage to the borrower's distinctive needs and circumstances. Of great importance, as well, is the state of interest rates at the time the mortgage is booked, renewed or refinanced.

One of the greatest advantages of long-term mortgages is the security they provide — "no need to worry about our mortgage for the next five years." With a fixed, low rate of interest and acceptable terms, it is the first choice of most home buyers and home owners. It puts to bed the fear of what will happen if rates rise in the next few years. The downside risks, though, are well known. A premium has to be paid by way of a higher interest rate; a penalty also may be incurred if the mortgage is to be prepaid before its maturity.

Shorter-term mortgages, the favorite when interest rates are high and borrowers believe the trend is downward, also have their advantages and disadvantages. By their nature, short-term mortgages "open up" more frequently than long-term mortgages. This is one way of dealing with abnormally high interest rates. Yet shorter-term mortgages are a gamble as well because the borrower assumes that interest rates will be lower when the mortgage term matures. What will happen, though, if rates are as high or higher when the mortgage matures? The going interest rate will have to be paid after maturity, and no one really knows what they will be at any given future date. Since lenders are not obligated to renew the mortgage, borrowers could face a serious crisis, as many did in 1981 and 1982, when interest rates skyrocketed. An existing lender might not be willing to renew, and new lenders might not be willing to refinance the loan, due to a rise in interest rates or a drop in real estate values.

Earlier, trying to decide where interest rates are going was called the biggest crap game in town. Even the experts admit they cannot predict where interest rates are going.

No easy answer exists. If trends tell anything, they indicate that most people want some security and are willing to pay for it. This has made the three-year loan the most popular in recent years. With more liberal prepayment privileges, longer-term commitments would be more acceptable. Yet the fringe element still does exist, those who continuously renew a six-month mortgage to beat the interest rates, and those who want long-term security and five-year mortgages, despite the price. The mortgage market is like a carnival — there is something out there for everyone!

40

Home, Sweet Home

An interesting phenomenon has been noted in recent years — a return to the old virtues. One of those virtues is to avoid living in debt. The interest generated recently in accelerating the retirement of mortgage debts is proof positive of this fact.

Years ago, when mortgages were fully paid off and discharged, borrowers held mortgage burning parties. Attaining 100% equity in the property was an important stage in life, and certainly cause for celebration. Are things really that much different today? Armed with this new-found knowledge, Canadian borrowers confidently can negotiate from strength, and need not accept merely what is presented to them. Armed with this new-found knowledge, Canadian borrowers can start playing the POPS game right away, employing some of the tricks explained earlier to reduce the high interest costs of mortgage financing.

The attitude of the public towards mortgages is changing. For years, when they were not fully understood, the only thing Canadians feared more than a mortgage was having to go out and arrange one. It's a different world today. Instead of fearing mortgages, Canadians now know what they are, how they work and how to pay them off sooner. Excitement surrounds the POPS game; just playing the game means winning big.

A toast — to the next mortgage burning party! It has been well deserved!

Appendix A

Checklist for Mortgage Clauses
1. What is the interest rate?
2. How often is it calculated (semi-annually? monthly?).
3. What is the term of the mortgage?
4. What is the amortization for the loan (this determines the monthly payment).
5. Does the lender maintain a realty tax account? Is interest payable, and if so, at what rate?
6. Are increased payments permitted?
7. Is the mortgage fully assumable if the property is sold? Is lender approval needed?
8. What are the prepayment privileges?
    (a) fully open;
    (b) open with a fixed penalty or notice;
    (c) limited open privilege — no penalty or notice;
    (d) limited open privilege — fixed penalty or notice;
    (e) fully closed;
    (f) combination of the above.
    What period of time applies to each category?

Other Factors

    i)   How much can be prepaid and what is the penalty?

    ii)   Is the privilege cumulative or noncumulative?

    iii)   Is there a minimum that must be prepaid?

    iv)   Must the amortization schedule be followed?

    v)   When is prepayment permitted?

    vi)   When does the prepayment privilege start?

    vii) What type of prepayment (lump sum vs. increased payment) is allowed?

    viii) Does the lender use "present value" prepayments?

9. Does the lender offer weekly/bi-weekly/semi-monthly payments?

10. What is the appraisal fee?

11. What is the maximum commitment period?

Appendix B

Amortization Schedule

Reference   SILVERSTEIN

Amount   50,000.00   Payment $ 551.20   Payable   MONTHLY   Print   TO MATURITY

First Payment Due   FEB 1 85   Rate 13.0000% Compounded SEMI-ANNUAL Interest Payment Factor .010551074

Payment Number	Payment Date	Total Payment	Interest Payment	Annual Interest Totals	Principal Payment	Annual Principal Totals	Balance of Loan
1	FEB 1 85	551.20	527.55		23.65		49,976.35
2	MAR 1 85	551.20	527.30		23.90		49,952.45
3	APR 1 85	551.20	527.05		24.15		49,928.30
4	MAY 1 85	551.20	526.80		24.40		49,903.90
5	JUN 1 85	551.20	526.54		24.66		49,879.24
6	JUL 1 85	551.20	526.28		24.92		49,854.32
7	AUG 1 85	551.20	526.02		25.18		49,829.14
8	SEP 1 85	551.20	525.75		25.45		49,803.69
9	OCT 1 85	551.20	525.48		25.72		49,777.97
10	NOV 1 85	551.20	525.21		25.99		49,751.98
11	DEC 1 85	551.20	524.94		26.26		49,725.72
				5,788.92		274.28	
12	JAN 1 86	551.20	524.66		26.54		49,699.18
13	FEB 1 86	551.20	524.38		26.82		49,672.36
14	MAR 1 86	551.20	524.10		27.10		49,645.26
15	APR 1 86	551.20	523.81		27.39		49,617.87
16	MAY 1 86	551.20	523.52		27.68		49,590.19
17	JUN 1 86	551.20	523.23		27.97		49,562.22
18	JUL 1 86	551.20	522.93		28.27		49,533.95
19	AUG 1 86	551.20	522.64		28.56		49,505.39
20	SEP 1 86	551.20	522.34		28.86		49,476.53
21	OCT 1 86	551.20	522.03		29.17		49,447.36
22	NOV 1 86	551.20	521.72		29.48		49,417.88
23	DEC 1 86	551.20	521.41		29.79		49,388.09
				6,276.77		337.63	
24	JAN 1 87	551.20	521.10		30.10		49,357.99
25	FEB 1 87	551.20	520.78		30.42		49,327.57
26	MAR 1 87	551.20	520.46		30.74		49,296.83
27	APR 1 87	551.20	520.13		31.07		49,265.76
28	MAY 1 87	551.20	519.81		31.39		49,234.37
29	JUN 1 87	551.20	519.48		31.72		49,202.65
30	JUL 1 87	551.20	519.14		32.06		49,170.59
31	AUG 1 87	551.20	518.80		32.40		49,138.19
32	SEP 1 87	551.20	518.46		32.74		49,105.45
33	OCT 1 87	551.20	518.12		33.08		49,072.37
34	NOV 1 87	551.20	517.77		33.43		49,038.94
35	DEC 1 87	551.20	517.41		33.79		49,005.15
				6,231.46		382.94	
36	JAN 1 88	551.20	517.06		34.14		48,971.01
37	FEB 1 88	551.20	516.70		34.50		48,936.51
38	MAR 1 88	551.20	516.33		34.87		48,901.64
39	APR 1 88	551.20	515.96		35.24		48,866.40
40	MAY 1 88	551.20	515.59		35.61		48,830.79
41	JUN 1 88	551.20	515.22		35.98		48,794.81
42	JUL 1 88	551.20	514.84		36.36		48,758.45
43	AUG 1 88	551.20	514.45		36.75		48,721.70
44	SEP 1 88	551.20	514.07		37.13		48,684.57
45	OCT 1 88	551.20	513.67		37.53		48,647.04
46	NOV 1 88	551.20	513.28		37.92		48,609.12
47	DEC 1 88	551.20	512.88		38.32		48,570.80
				6,180.05		434.35	
48	JAN 1 89	551.20	512.47		38.73		48,532.07
49	FEB 1 89	551.20	512.07		39.13		48,492.94
50	MAR 1 89	551.20	511.65		39.55		48,453.39
51	APR 1 89	551.20	511.24		39.96		48,413.43
52	MAY 1 89	551.20	510.81		40.39		48,373.04
53	JUN 1 89	551.20	510.39		40.81		48,332.23
54	JUL 1 89	551.20	509.96		41.24		48,290.99
55	AUG 1 89	551.20	509.52		41.68		48,249.31
56	SEP 1 89	551.20	509.08		42.12		48,207.19
57	OCT 1 89	551.20	508.64		42.56		48,164.63
58	NOV 1 89	551.20	508.19		43.01		48,121.62
59	DEC 1 89	551.20	507.73		43.47		48,078.15
				6,121.75		492.65	
60	JAN 1 90	551.20	507.28		43.92		48,034.23

Reference   SILVERSTEIN

Amount   50,000.00   Payment $ 551.20   Payable   MONTHLY   Print   TO MATURITY

First Payment Due   FEB 1 85   Rate 13.0000% Compounded SEMI-ANNUAL Interest Payment Factor   .010551074

Payment Number	Payment Date			Total Payment	Interest Payment	Annual Interest Totals	Principal Payment	Annual Principal Totals	Balance of Loan
61	FEB	1	90	551.20	506.81		44.39		47,989.84
62	MAR	1	90	551.20	506.34		44.86		47,944.98
63	APR	1	90	551.20	505.87		45.33		47,899.65
64	MAY	1	90	551.20	505.39		45.81		47,853.84
65	JUN	1	90	551.20	504.91		46.29		47,807.55
66	JUL	1	90	551.20	504.42		46.78		47,760.77
67	AUG	1	90	551.20	503.93		47.27		47,713.50
68	SEP	1	90	551.20	503.43		47.77		47,665.73
69	OCT	1	90	551.20	502.92		48.28		47,617.45
70	NOV	1	90	551.20	502.42		48.78		47,568.67
71	DEC	1	90	551.20	501.90		49.30		47,519.37
						6,055.62		558.78	
72	JAN	1	91	551.20	501.38		49.82		47,469.55
73	FEB	1	91	551.20	500.85		50.35		47,419.20
74	MAR	1	91	551.20	500.32		50.88		47,368.32
75	APR	1	91	551.20	499.79		51.41		47,316.91
76	MAY	1	91	551.20	499.24		51.96		47,264.95
77	JUN	1	91	551.20	498.70		52.50		47,212.45
78	JUL	1	91	551.20	498.14		53.06		47,159.39
79	AUG	1	91	551.20	497.58		53.62		47,105.77
80	SEP	1	91	551.20	497.02		54.18		47,051.59
81	OCT	1	91	551.20	496.44		54.76		46,996.83
82	NOV	1	91	551.20	495.87		55.33		46,941.50
83	DEC	1	91	551.20	495.28		55.92		46,885.58
						5,980.61		633.79	
84	JAN	1	92	551.20	494.69		56.51		46,829.07
85	FEB	1	92	551.20	494.10		57.10		46,771.97
86	MAR	1	92	551.20	493.49		57.71		46,714.26
87	APR	1	92	551.20	492.89		58.31		46,655.95
88	MAY	1	92	551.20	492.27		58.93		46,597.02
89	JUN	1	92	551.20	491.65		59.55		46,537.47
90	JUL	1	92	551.20	491.02		60.18		46,477.29
91	AUG	1	92	551.20	490.39		60.81		46,416.48
92	SEP	1	92	551.20	489.74		61.46		46,355.02
93	OCT	1	92	551.20	489.10		62.10		46,292.92
94	NOV	1	92	551.20	488.44		62.76		46,230.16
95	DEC	1	92	551.20	487.78		63.42		46,166.74
						5,895.56		718.84	
96	JAN	1	93	551.20	487.11		64.09		46,102.65
97	FEB	1	93	551.20	486.43		64.77		46,037.88
98	MAR	1	93	551.20	485.75		65.45		45,972.43
99	APR	1	93	551.20	485.06		66.14		45,906.29
100	MAY	1	93	551.20	484.36		66.84		45,839.45
101	JUN	1	93	551.20	483.66		67.54		45,771.91
102	JUL	1	93	551.20	482.94		68.26		45,703.65
103	AUG	1	93	551.20	482.22		68.98		45,634.67
104	SEP	1	93	551.20	481.49		69.71		45,564.96
105	OCT	1	93	551.20	480.76		70.44		45,494.52
106	NOV	1	93	551.20	480.02		71.18		45,423.34
107	DEC	1	93	551.20	479.27		71.93		45,351.41
						5,799.07		815.33	
108	JAN	1	94	551.20	478.51		72.69		45,278.72
109	FEB	1	94	551.20	477.74		73.46		45,205.26
110	MAR	1	94	551.20	476.96		74.24		45,131.02
111	APR	1	94	551.20	476.18		75.02		45,056.00
112	MAY	1	94	551.20	475.39		75.81		44,980.19
113	JUN	1	94	551.20	474.59		76.61		44,903.58
114	JUL	1	94	551.20	473.78		77.42		44,826.16
115	AUG	1	94	551.20	472.96		78.24		44,747.92
116	SEP	1	94	551.20	472.14		79.06		44,668.86
117	OCT	1	94	551.20	471.30		79.90		44,588.96
118	NOV	1	94	551.20	470.46		80.74		44,508.22
119	DEC	1	94	551.20	469.61		81.59		44,426.63
						5,689.62		924.78	
120	JAN	1	95	551.20	468.75		82.45		44,344.18

Reference	SILVERSTEIN						
Amount	50,000.00	Payment $ 551.20	Payable	MONTHLY	Print	TO MATURITY	
First Payment Due	FEB 1 85	Rate 13.0000% Compounded SEMI-ANNUAL	Interest Payment Factor	.010551074			

Payment Number	Payment Date	Total Payment	Interest Payment	Annual Interest Totals	Principal Payment	Annual Principal Totals	Balance of Loan
121	FEB 1 95	551.20	467.88		83.32		44,260.86
122	MAR 1 95	551.20	467.00		84.20		44,176.66
123	APR 1 95	551.20	466.11		85.09		44,091.57
124	MAY 1 95	551.20	465.21		85.99		44,005.58
125	JUN 1 95	551.20	464.31		86.89		43,918.69
126	JUL 1 95	551.20	463.39		87.81		43,830.88
127	AUG 1 95	551.20	462.46		88.74		43,742.14
128	SEP 1 95	551.20	461.53		89.67		43,652.47
129	OCT 1 95	551.20	460.58		90.62		43,561.85
130	NOV 1 95	551.20	459.62		91.58		43,470.27
131	DEC 1 95	551.20	458.66	5,565.50	92.54	1,048.90	43,377.73
132	JAN 1 96	551.20	457.68		93.52		43,284.21
133	FEB 1 96	551.20	456.69		94.51		43,189.70
134	MAR 1 96	551.20	455.70		95.50		43,094.20
135	APR 1 96	551.20	454.69		96.51		42,997.69
136	MAY 1 96	551.20	453.67		97.53		42,900.16
137	JUN 1 96	551.20	452.64		98.56		42,801.60
138	JUL 1 96	551.20	451.60		99.60		42,702.00
139	AUG 1 96	551.20	450.55		100.65		42,601.35
140	SEP 1 96	551.20	449.49		101.71		42,499.64
141	OCT 1 96	551.20	448.42		102.78		42,396.86
142	NOV 1 96	551.20	447.33		103.87		42,292.99
143	DEC 1 96	551.20	446.24	5,424.70	104.96	1,189.70	42,188.03
144	JAN 1 97	551.20	445.13		106.07		42,081.96
145	FEB 1 97	551.20	444.01		107.19		41,974.77
146	MAR 1 97	551.20	442.88		108.32		41,866.45
147	APR 1 97	551.20	441.74		109.46		41,756.99
148	MAY 1 97	551.20	440.58		110.62		41,646.37
149	JUN 1 97	551.20	439.41		111.79		41,534.58
150	JUL 1 97	551.20	438.23		112.97		41,421.61
151	AUG 1 97	551.20	437.04		114.16		41,307.45
152	SEP 1 97	551.20	435.84		115.36		41,192.09
153	OCT 1 97	551.20	434.62		116.58		41,075.51
154	NOV 1 97	551.20	433.39		117.81		40,957.70
155	DEC 1 97	551.20	432.15	5,265.02	119.05	1,349.38	40,838.65
156	JAN 1 98	551.20	430.89		120.31		40,718.34
157	FEB 1 98	551.20	429.62		121.58		40,596.76
158	MAR 1 98	551.20	428.34		122.86		40,473.90
159	APR 1 98	551.20	427.04		124.16		40,349.74
160	MAY 1 98	551.20	425.73		125.47		40,224.27
161	JUN 1 98	551.20	424.41		126.79		40,097.48
162	JUL 1 98	551.20	423.07		128.13		39,969.35
163	AUG 1 98	551.20	421.72		129.48		39,839.87
164	SEP 1 98	551.20	420.35		130.85		39,709.02
165	OCT 1 98	551.20	418.97		132.23		39,576.79
166	NOV 1 98	551.20	417.58		133.62		39,443.17
167	DEC 1 98	551.20	416.17	5,083.89	135.03	1,530.51	39,308.14
168	JAN 1 99	551.20	414.74		136.46		39,171.68
169	FEB 1 99	551.20	413.30		137.90		39,033.78
170	MAR 1 99	551.20	411.85		139.35		38,894.43
171	APR 1 99	551.20	410.38		140.82		38,753.61
172	MAY 1 99	551.20	408.89		142.31		38,611.30
173	JUN 1 99	551.20	407.39		143.81		38,467.49
174	JUL 1 99	551.20	405.87		145.33		38,322.16
175	AUG 1 99	551.20	404.34		146.86		38,175.30
176	SEP 1 99	551.20	402.79		148.41		38,026.89
177	OCT 1 99	551.20	401.22		149.98		37,876.91
178	NOV 1 99	551.20	399.64		151.56		37,725.35
179	DEC 1 99	551.20	398.04	4,878.45	153.16	1,735.95	37,572.19
180	JAN 1 00	551.20	396.43		154.77		37,417.42

Reference   SILVERSTEIN

Amount   50,000.00   Payment $ 551.20   Payable   MONTHLY   Print   TO MATURITY

First Payment Due   FEB 1 85   Rate 13.0000%   Compounds : SEMI-ANNUAL   Interest Payment Factor   .010551074

Payment Number	Payment Date			Total Payment	Interest Payment	Annual Interest Totals	Principal Payment	Annual Principal Totals	Balance of Loan
181	FEB	1	00	551.20	394.79		156.41		37,261.01
182	MAR	1	00	551.20	393.14		158.06		37,102.95
183	APR	1	00	551.20	391.48		159.72		36,943.23
184	MAY	1	00	551.20	389.79		161.41		36,781.82
185	JUN	1	00	551.20	388.09		163.11		36,618.71
186	JUL	1	00	551.20	386.37		164.83		36,453.88
187	AUG	1	00	551.20	384.63		166.57		36,287.31
188	SEP	1	00	551.20	382.87		168.33		36,118.98
189	OCT	1	00	551.20	381.09		170.11		35,948.87
190	NOV	1	00	551.20	379.30		171.90		35,776.97
191	DEC	1	00	551.20	377.49		173.71		35,603.26
						4,645.47		1,968.93	
192	JAN	1	1	551.20	375.65		175.55		35,427.71
193	FEB	1	1	551.20	373.80		177.40		35,250.31
194	MAR	1	1	551.20	371.93		179.27		35,071.04
195	APR	1	1	551.20	370.04		181.16		34,889.88
196	MAY	1	1	551.20	368.13		183.07		34,706.81
197	JUN	1	1	551.20	366.19		185.01		34,521.80
198	JUL	1	1	551.20	364.24		186.96		34,334.84
199	AUG	1	1	551.20	362.27		188.93		34,145.91
200	SEP	1	1	551.20	360.28		190.92		33,954.99
201	OCT	1	1	551.20	358.26		192.94		33,762.05
202	NOV	1	1	551.20	356.23		194.97		33,567.08
203	DEC	1	1	551.20	354.17		197.03		33,370.05
						4,381.19		2,233.21	
204	JAN	1	2	551.20	352.09		199.11		33,170.94
205	FEB	1	2	551.20	349.99		201.21		32,969.73
206	MAR	1	2	551.20	347.87		203.33		32,766.40
207	APR	1	2	551.20	345.72		205.48		32,560.92
208	MAY	1	2	551.20	343.55		207.65		32,353.27
209	JUN	1	2	551.20	341.36		209.84		32,143.43
210	JUL	1	2	551.20	339.15		212.05		31,931.38
211	AUG	1	2	551.20	336.91		214.29		31,717.09
212	SEP	1	2	551.20	334.65		216.55		31,500.54
213	OCT	1	2	551.20	332.36		218.84		31,281.70
214	NOV	1	2	551.20	330.06		221.14		31,060.56
215	DEC	1	2	551.20	327.72		223.48		30,837.08
						4,081.43		2,532.97	
216	JAN	1	3	551.20	325.36		225.84		30,611.24
217	FEB	1	3	551.20	322.98		228.22		30,383.02
218	MAR	1	3	551.20	320.57		230.63		30,152.39
219	APR	1	3	551.20	318.14		233.06		29,919.33
220	MAY	1	3	551.20	315.68		235.52		29,683.81
221	JUN	1	3	551.20	313.20		238.00		29,445.81
222	JUL	1	3	551.20	310.68		240.52		29,205.29
223	AUG	1	3	551.20	308.15		243.05		28,962.24
224	SEP	1	3	551.20	305.58		245.62		28,716.62
225	OCT	1	3	551.20	302.99		248.21		28,468.41
226	NOV	1	3	551.20	300.37		250.83		28,217.58
227	DEC	1	3	551.20	297.73		253.47		27,964.11
						3,741.43		2,872.97	
228	JAN	1	4	551.20	295.05		256.15		27,707.96
229	FEB	1	4	551.20	292.35		258.85		27,449.11
230	MAR	1	4	551.20	289.62		261.58		27,187.53
231	APR	1	4	551.20	286.86		264.34		26,923.19
232	MAY	1	4	551.20	284.07		267.13		26,656.06
233	JUN	1	4	551.20	281.25		269.95		26,386.11
234	JUL	1	4	551.20	278.40		272.80		26,113.31
235	AUG	1	4	551.20	275.52		275.68		25,837.63
236	SEP	1	4	551.20	272.61		278.59		25,559.04
237	OCT	1	4	551.20	269.68		281.52		25,277.52
238	NOV	1	4	551.20	266.70		284.50		24,993.02
239	DEC	1	4	551.20	263.70		287.50		24,705.52
						3,355.81		3,258.59	
240	JAN	1	5	551.20	260.67		290.53		24,414.99

| Reference | SILVERSTEIN | | | | | | | |

Amount   50,000.00   Payment $ 551.20 Payable MONTHLY Print TO MATURITY

First Payment Due FEB 1 85 Rate 13.0000% Compounded SEMI-ANNUAL Interest Payment Factor .010551074

Payment Number	Payment Date			Total Payment	Interest Payment	Annual Interest Totals	Principal Payment	Annual Principal Totals	Balance of Loan
241	FEB	1	5	551.20	257.60		293.60		24,121.39
242	MAR	1	5	551.20	254.51		296.69		23,824.70
243	APR	1	5	551.20	251.38		299.82		23,524.88
244	MAY	1	5	551.20	248.21		302.99		23,221.89
245	JUN	1	5	551.20	245.02		306.18		22,915.71
246	JUL	1	5	551.20	241.79		309.41		22,606.30
247	AUG	1	5	551.20	238.52		312.68		22,293.62
248	SEP	1	5	551.20	235.22		315.98		21,977.64
249	OCT	1	5	551.20	231.89		319.31		21,658.33
250	NOV	1	5	551.20	228.52		322.68		21,335.65
251	DEC	1	5	551.20	225.11		326.09		21,009.56
						2,918.44		3,695.96	
252	JAN	1	6	551.20	221.67		329.53		20,680.03
253	FEB	1	6	551.20	218.20		333.00		20,347.03
254	MAR	1	6	551.20	214.68		336.52		20,010.51
255	APR	1	6	551.20	211.13		340.07		19,670.44
256	MAY	1	6	551.20	207.54		343.66		19,326.78
257	JUN	1	6	551.20	203.92		347.28		18,979.50
258	JUL	1	6	551.20	200.25		350.95		18,628.55
259	AUG	1	6	551.20	196.55		354.65		18,273.90
260	SEP	1	6	551.20	192.81		358.39		17,915.51
261	OCT	1	6	551.20	189.03		362.17		17,553.34
262	NOV	1	6	551.20	185.21		365.99		17,187.35
263	DEC	1	6	551.20	181.35		369.85		16,817.50
						2,422.34		4,192.06	
264	JAN	1	7	551.20	177.44		373.76		16,443.74
265	FEB	1	7	551.20	173.50		377.70		16,066.04
266	MAR	1	7	551.20	169.51		381.69		15,684.35
267	APR	1	7	551.20	165.49		385.71		15,298.64
268	MAY	1	7	551.20	161.42		389.78		14,908.86
269	JUN	1	7	551.20	157.30		393.90		14,514.96
270	JUL	1	7	551.20	153.15		398.05		14,116.91
271	AUG	1	7	551.20	148.95		402.25		13,714.66
272	SEP	1	7	551.20	144.70		406.50		13,308.16
273	OCT	1	7	551.20	140.42		410.78		12,897.38
274	NOV	1	7	551.20	136.08		415.12		12,482.26
275	DEC	1	7	551.20	131.70		419.50		12,062.76
						1,859.66		4,754.74	
276	JAN	1	8	551.20	127.28		423.92		11,638.84
277	FEB	1	8	551.20	122.80		428.40		11,210.44
278	MAR	1	8	551.20	118.28		432.92		10,777.52
279	APR	1	8	551.20	113.71		437.49		10,340.03
280	MAY	1	8	551.20	109.10		442.10		9,897.93
281	JUN	1	8	551.20	104.43		446.77		9,451.16
282	JUL	1	8	551.20	99.72		451.48		8,999.68
283	AUG	1	8	551.20	94.96		456.24		8,543.44
284	SEP	1	8	551.20	90.14		461.06		8,082.38
285	OCT	1	8	551.20	85.28		465.92		7,616.46
286	NOV	1	8	551.20	80.36		470.84		7,145.62
287	DEC	1	8	551.20	75.39		475.81		6,669.81
						1,221.45		5,392.95	
288	JAN	1	9	551.20	70.37		480.83		6,188.98
289	FEB	1	9	551.20	65.30		485.90		5,703.08
290	MAR	1	9	551.20	60.17		491.03		5,212.05
291	APR	1	9	551.20	54.99		496.21		4,715.84
292	MAY	1	9	551.20	49.76		501.44		4,214.40
293	JUN	1	9	551.20	44.47		506.73		3,707.67
294	JUL	1	9	551.20	39.12		512.08		3,195.59
295	AUG	1	9	551.20	33.72		517.48		2,678.11
296	SEP	1	9	551.20	28.26		522.94		2,155.17
297	OCT	1	9	551.20	22.74		528.46		1,626.71
298	NOV	1	9	551.20	17.16		534.04		1,092.67
299	DEC	1	9	551.20	11.53		539.67		553.00
						497.59		6,116.81	
300	JAN	1	10	551.20	5.83		545.37		7.63
301	FEB	1	10	7.71	.08	5.91	7.63	553.00	.00

The Amortization Schedule was supplied courtesy of MCR Mortgage
Services, Toronto, Canada